That Perfect Spring

Bruce Fabricant

ISBN: 978-0-578-01534-7

Cover photo:
A.B. Davis High School 1959 championship baseball team: Front row, left to right: Ed Whitman, photographer, Steve Matthews, Len Henderson, Bruce Fabricant, Frank Fiore, Neil Arena, equipment managers Louis Kurtzberg and Gary Vezzoli. Rear row, equipment manager Art Eisenberg, Bob Puccillo, Nick Giordano, Tony Cioppa, Eddie Martin, Teddy Cardasis, Richard Giloth, Ernie Motta, Tommy Ambrosino, and John Fortier. Missing are Mike Abrams, Richie Shapiro, Jimmy Gross, Charlie Siegel, and equipment manager Billy Cioppa.

For Bobbi, Robin, Vicki, Morris and Vera

Acknowledgments

I would like to take this opportunity to thank the people whose generosity, cooperation, advice, assistance, and encouragement made this journey back to the spring of 1959 possible.

Susan Zanjani, a dear friend in California, for her editorial stewardship and her red pen that was at work throughout the entire project.

Eddie Martin for thinking this was worth doing in the first place and for being there every step of the way.

Steve Matthews for being my lifetime teammate since 1947.

Paul Court, who has taught in the Mount Vernon school system for nearly 30 years, for his background about the city and the history of the high school on the Gramatan Avenue hilltop.

Lou Berman and Carl Lundquist, wherever you are.

Above all, I wish to express my heart-felt thanks to my 14 teammates who so generously shared their memories with me and allowed me to use pictures from their personal albums.

Contents

Introduction

This is a book about what it was like to grow up and play baseball in Mount Vernon, New York, during the 1950s. It is about how a group of juniors and seniors at Mount Vernon's A.B. Davis High School came together for one glorious season in 1959 to win the Westchester Interscholastic Athletic Association baseball championship (12-3-1). But the book is much more than that. It is about their hopes, triumphs, and failures in a game learned at the hands of their fathers, brothers, and even mothers on Union Avenue, Valois Place, North Tenth and South Twelfth Avenues, and playgrounds throughout the city. It is about the excitement of buying a first baseball mitt at Tom Godfrey's sporting goods store on Fourth Avenue, feeling fear on a cold spring morning when trying out for the Little League at Hutchinson Field, and singing songs on long bus rides to high school road games.

It is about Eddie Martin, Westchester's best right hander, compiling one of the finest season-long pitching performances in school history. It is about Tommy Ambrosino and Teddy Cardasis batting their way to All-County honors. It is about Neil Arena telling how his cobbler father repaired Lou Gehrig's shoes.

Fifty baseball seasons have come and gone since '59. A. B. Davis High School does not exist any more. It is now Mount Vernon High School and basketball rules. But the memories and recollections of 15 players from that team have not diminished even though time is pushing them closer and closer to 70 years of age. Two teammates are deceased, Richie Shapiro and Richard Giloth, as well as equipment manager Billy Cioppa. Sixteen players survive along with equipment managers Gary Vezzoli and Lou Kurtzberg. Fifteen of the sixteen players were eager to reminisce.

It has been said that 'The best part of baseball is the past.' So these are their stories, told in their words. They talk with enthusiasm and love about their early years in Mount Vernon. To a man, they discussed living in an idealized past, a past without pain and complexity. I can only assume that that championship season has been a major highlight of their athletic lives. They speak with joy about it. They are proud of what they accomplished. The A.B. Davis Hilltoppers wasn't a great team. But we were winners at the highest level of Westchester County baseball.

Had A.B. Davis High School not won that championship, beating teams from New Rochelle, White Plains, and Yonkers, I would not have written this book. That championship has been our bond. I've often looked back with fondness to those 49 spring days of baseball in 1959. I have also found myself wondering about where my teammates were and how life has treated them. They are scattered far and wide. They call places like Durham, Connecticut: Naples, Florida: Argyle, New York, and even the Bahamas, home. The internet is a wonderful tool. It helped locate many teammates I had not heard from in nearly 50 years.

The inspiration for this book was Lawrence Ritter's classic *The Glory of Their Times*. Ritter took a tape recorder, asked questions, and listened to major leaguers who played 50, 60, and almost 70 years earlier. Their stories were told in their words. I did the same thing with my teammates. I transported them back to 1959 and even earlier. I talked to them in restaurants, diners, business offices, in their homes, and on the telephone. I asked them what it was like in the mid-1950s in Mount Vernon. I didn't know what the outcome would be. I found a group of men who were eager to talk about the city they grew up in and their earliest baseball recollections. All I had to do was listen. So this book really wasn't written. It was spoken. All my teammates had to do was remember a championship that came with little foreshadowing, and talk about one season, at least, when A.B. Davis High School outshined everyone. And when we got together and talked we remained forever young.

So come back with me to 1959 and listen how we played baseball in Mount Vernon with a joy that's seldom seen.

Bruce Fabricant

2009

A.B. Davis High School 1959

Catchers

	1959 Address
Cioppa (Tony)	432 South First Avenue

Infielders

	Position	1959 Address
Abrams (Mike)	third base	82 Sheridan Avenue
Ambrosino (Tom)	first base	23 North Tenth Avenue
Arena (Neil)	second base shortstop	131 South Twelfth Avenue
Fabricant (Bruce)	second base	44 Fleetwood Avenue
Fiore (Frank)	shortstop	21 West Sydney Avenue
Gross (Jimmy)	second base	15 Lexington Avenue
Matthews (Steve)	first base	25 Brookfield Road

Outfielders

	Position	1959 Address
Cardasis, (Ted)	center field first base	41 East Grand Street
Fortier, (John)	center field	445 Gramatan Avenue
Giloth, (Richard)	center field	Locust Street
Giordano, (Nick)	left field	442 North High Street
Henderson, (Lenny)	right field	26 Union Avenue

Pitchers

	Position	1959 Address
Martin, (Eddie)	pitcher (rh)	2 Valois Place
Motta, (Ernie)	pitcher (rh)	454 South Seventh Avenue
Puccillo, (Bob)	pitcher (rh)	123 Beachwood Avenue
Siegel, (Charlie)	pitcher (lh)	8 Hartley Avenue
Shapiro, Richie	pitcher (rh)	Commonwealth Avenue

Coach

Sywetz, (Bill)

Eddie Martin.

1 *Eddie Martin*

A good case can be made that Eddie Martin's pitching exploits in 1959 was the greatest single season performance in A.B. Davis High School's history. He was 7-0. He started eight games and completed all his winning starts. Under continuous low scoring game pressure, he threw three shutouts along with a 1-0 no-hitter against New Rochelle. In between starts, he played shortstop and led the club in games played, at bats, runs scored and triples. The Westchester County Publishers Inc. selected him as the county's outstanding right-handed pitcher.

My father's name was Edward. He was the first Edward. I'm the second, and one of my sons is also Edward. It makes it very confusing.

My mother, Bertha, was part of a family from Mount Vernon dating back more than 125 years. I found my great grandfather's obituary. He was born in Rome, NY, in 1847 and moved at an early age to Manhattan. He was in the oil business and then moved to Mount Vernon in the 1880s where he established a contracting business. Supposedly, he paved many of the roads in Mount Vernon that are still there.

So you can say Mount Vernon has been in our family for a long time. I was born in Mount Vernon Hospital. But to be really technical, my parents had an apartment on 233rd Street in the Bronx. My earliest recollection was moving to Union Avenue in Mt. Vernon. I only have a glimmer of that.

My parents then moved to the house on Valois Place where I

lived until I was married. This was in the most northeastern part of Mount Vernon called Chester Heights, an area that encompasses portions of Eastchester, Pelham, New Rochelle and Mount Vernon. The house might have been small, but it was a great home. It dead-ended into the Hutchinson River Parkway. Behind our backyard were woods.

It seemed when I was six and seven and growing up in Chester Heights, it was unusual that a house there did not have at least one youngster in it. With the woods behind us, and a couple of vacant lots that aren't vacant now, there was always a wood basketball backboard there. If it wasn't basketball, it was punch ball and stick ball.

It was a great place to grow up in.

My dad was in the monument business. His family, his grandfather and his grandfather's cousin established quite a monument business. When Woodlawn Cemetery opened in the Bronx, shortly after the Civil War, my great grandfather and his cousin did quite a few of the monuments for soldiers who died in the Civil War. I understand they were working on the United States Capital in Washington DC when the Civil War broke out. They had to come home as the war increased and construction stopped. Eventually they split up and my great grandfather opened a monument business right outside of Kensico Cemetery in Valhalla when Kensico opened up.

As a coincidence, the War Dog Memorial at America's oldest pet cemetery, Hartsdale Pet Cemetery, was designed by my great grandfather's cousin who was originally a partner in Robert Caterson. Caterson is my middle name.

I can't pinpoint when I started playing baseball. I was the youngest cousin in our family. They played a lot of ball with me in the backyard, in the woods behind our house. In the Eastchester portion of Chester Heights, there was a ball field next to a fire house. They would take me up there.

In the backyard of the house there was a huge foundation because the house was close to the water and needed to be elevated. That wall made a perfect place to throw a ball against. I threw against it all day long. I would play little games with myself, like figuring out which brick to hit. Not only would I try to hit a specific stone on that wall, but when the ball bounced back it would help me practice my fielding. I didn't think of it as practice. I thought it was just fun.

Everybody in the family followed baseball. They were New York Yankees fans. Somehow I liked the Brooklyn Dodgers. My older cousin would tease me unmercifully. We would play games where my cousin would be the Yankees, and I would be the Dodgers. I lost all the time.

Jackie Robinson was my hero. No one came close to him in my mind. My father took me to Ebbets Field I think the first year Jackie played in 1947. All I remember was seeing Robinson leading off a base, stealing, and running around. Of course, another thing was that Ralph Branca came from Mount Vernon and was on the Dodgers. I recall when they loaded a bunch of us kids on a bus and took us down to Ralph Branca Day at Ebbets Field.

My father and I played catch a lot whenever he could. He was a quite an athlete but not a baseball player. His sports were swimming and track. He went to Horace Mann School in Riverdale. When he passed on and we cleaned out the house that they lived in for 50 years, I found his yearbooks from Horace Mann, and there he was, running track and swimming. He was interested in baseball and sensed that I was tremendously interested in it as well.

I would say my father certainly didn't push me. Let's put it this way. I pushed myself. You see, everybody was playing baseball then. All of my relatives lived on the south side of Mount Vernon. I've often talked to people about this. I would take the D bus from the middle of Mount Vernon near City Hall and the movie theatres. That bus would go east on Third Street into Pelham and then dead end in Chester Heights where it was the last stop. Looking out the bus window I saw quite a few vacant lots. Everybody was playing ball, mostly softball.

Eddie Martin: "It was unbelievable how accurate he was. He worked fast on the mound. It was one pitch after another; bing, bing, bing."

I had sort of a unique experience as far as friends were concerned when I was young. Initially, I had two distinct groups of friends. Shortly after I started playing Little League, I had three distinct groups of friends.

The Chester Heights neighborhood I grew up in was lower middle-class. There were all private houses. Most of the kids my age, boys and girls, went to parochial school. I went to the church that was in our area, but the parochial school, St. Catherine's, was in Pelham. I went to Wilson Elementary School which later became Traphagen Elementary and Junior High School.

We were way ahead of our times. We were bused to Traphagen where there were very few of the guys from the neighborhood. So I had another group of friends there during the daytime, like Jimmy Gross, Dickie Merbaum, Bob Levine and older guys like Ron Ceisler. We played informal games in the gym or during lunch time or after school.

I don't know why, and don't ask me why, because I never played the position, but my first glove somehow was a first baseman's mitt. We called it a Trapper's mitt then.

I distinctly remember going with my father into Pelham which was much closer to us than downtown Mount Vernon. There was a stationery/toy/sporting goods store on Fifth Avenue in Pelham. Why I got this first baseman's mitt I don't have the slightest idea. But I do remember buying it and the fun I had walking through the store and finally selecting the glove.

When I got older I bought my glove with my parents at Allen's Sporting Goods in New Rochelle. And then, of course, Tom Godfrey's in Mount Vernon became the sporting goods store of choice.

I think everyone remembers their first Little League experience. My first tryout was at Hutchinson Field, the same field we played ball on in high school. I was ecstatic when my folks showed me the application in the Mount Vernon Daily Argus. It sounded great.

I went down to Hutchinson Field. I was the only one from my neighborhood who tried out. You see, most of the guys from Traphagen went to summer camp. I don't remember anybody from school trying out. I took the bus from Chester Heights to Hutchinson Field. It was early spring and freezing cold.

They put numbers on our back. I tried out as a pitcher. At that time, in 1950, I was nine years old. The field seemed massive. Kids lined up and someone would say, "Number 14 get up at bat."

You had three shots at bat, and took three ground balls. That was it. After the tryout, I received a postcard in the mail telling me that I was on a team, but there was no name of the team at that point.

The thing was that they had four teams of possibly 18 to 20 kids on a team. The team was going to wind up with 15 players. So there were going to be cuts from the initial selection. For the first practice, and I think there were only two or three practices or initial tryouts, I remember going down to the small field located at Memorial Field, underneath the handball courts.

I didn't know anybody there. I was a little intimidated because most of the kids on the team were older than me. Many of them knew each other because they went to school together. The kids were mostly from the south side or west side of Mount Vernon, the Nichols Junior High School area. We voted to select the name of the team which would be called the Panthers.

I remember being completely dominated by a fellow who I am very friendly with now, Ralph Merigliano. He was the pitcher and, of course, when I got up to face him, I couldn't get the bat around. I couldn't do anything. Ralph eventually went to Edison Tech and became a Westchester All County third baseman.

I then received a postcard with the news I was cut from the team and became upset because, in my opinion, I thought I was better than a number of kids who made the team. I was upset because some of those kids had fathers who were coaches or involved with the league. I didn't cry. That was my first introduction to politics.

After being cut I asked my parents to take me to some Little League games. I vowed I would eventually make the team. When I made the Little League the next year on a different team called The Shamrocks, I thought I shouldn't try out for pitcher since the best players went out for pitcher. So I went out for second base.

I played Little League for three years. And it was tremendous fun. I remember getting on the D bus again in Chester Heights and taking it into the heart of Mount Vernon. Then I got on another bus called The Creek bus and went down South Fifth Avenue, getting off at Longfellow School.

Once again I was lucky enough to have a friend at Traphagen, Peter Rothenberg, who accompanied me there a couple of times the first year since I was intimidated. Of course, I knew absolutely no one there. As far as meeting people, it was a little worse.

Eddie Martin: "In our backyard there was a foundation wall that was a perfect place to throw a ball against. I had little games with myself, like figuring out which brick to hit."

Most of the guys had been on the team the prior year. There might have been five or six new kids added to the club. Once again, I think I was still the youngest on the team. I can still remember them. First place was shared by two pitchers; one was JJ Falco who went to A.B. Davis and played football and baseball. He was a big guy. He is no longer with us. Second base was another Davis graduate, Fred Casucci. Another fellow who had a very good career at Davis, Charley Sundberg, was the shortstop.

He also pitched. The third baseman was Bruce Leaf. The outfield was comprised of Joey Orlando, Nick Briglia, and me. The catcher was Johnny Robinson. We won the championship that year.

My folks didn't come watch me play in the beginning. And it wasn't because they weren't interested. Somehow, one of my distant relatives, who my mother grew up with in Mount Vernon, had a son who played on The Indians. His mother was active in the Mount Vernon Woman's Auxiliary. She got my mother involved in the organization. They both came to the games.

I went out for the A.B. Davis Junior Varsity team in my sophomore year, and our coach Cliff Tatro, an English teacher, started me in the season opener against Mount St. Michael in the Bronx. I knew Mount St. Michael was a pretty good team. I was friends with many players on that team. We won the game.

The next thing I knew, Davis' varsity baseball coach, Irv Halstead, contacted me and told me to come to the varsity practices from now on, which I did. At first I was honored to do that. However, it wasn't a great experience. I pitched in the next varsity game.

Looking back at it now, I understand what happened. I was taking someone's place on the mound who was a junior or senior. The team didn't take too kindly to that. I remember standing around shortstop on Howard Field behind the high school during batting practice.

The next thing I knew balls were flying in from the outfield and landing right next to me. Luckily, I wasn't hit. I knew two of the guys firing balls in. One was the pitcher who I replaced and the other was his friend, JJ Falco. Both were laughing. You see, I was the only sophomore on the team. It really bothered me. I got sick that year. It might have been the German measles. So I pitched three or four games, and I think I was 2-1.

I was back on the varsity as a junior. But this was a terrible year. Irv Halstead was still coaching. Subsequent to my baseball career, Mr. Halstead became a tremendous guy, supporting me in a number of ways. But during my junior season, maybe it was his style, he was very rough on me.

I distinctly remember pitching a game against Sleepy Hollow. During the game, Sleepy Hollow players stole quite a few bases. My catcher, who I knew as far back as Little League, was a nice guy, a friend of mine, an excellent receiver. But he didn't have a strong throwing arm.

After Sleepy Hollow stole its third base, Coach Halstead came out and ripped into me on the mound. I didn't take kindly to that. I didn't say anything to him. That was the last game I pitched for him. I didn't go to practice after that. I don't think I would have gone out for baseball in my senior year 1959, our championship season, if Irv Halstead was still coaching.

You know what made our 1959 club so special? I don't remember any "hot dogs" on the team. Everybody on the team that I was aware of wanted to win. Everyone wanted to hustle. They gave it everything they had.

We could use all the clichés, "small ball" or whatever. I think, after a couple of games, everybody realized that we could win and that we could beat anybody. Once that takes over a team, it becomes a positive thing.

I don't remember any arguments. No one balled anyone out. In his own way, Coach Sywetz did the right thing. He left us alone. He didn't humiliate anybody on the team. A lot of our teammates came to games and they didn't get in to play. They kept on coming. They were part of the team.

It's been 50 years and I remember some of our teammates better than others. Neil Arena I knew from Little League and from playing basketball. I remember playing ball against Tony Cioppa.

Again, the thing that stands out is that we weren't hot dogs. We had confidence. The guys hit the ball. They knew what to do. It seems to me that mostly everybody, if not everyone, had very good baseball sense. That might be taking the extra base or getting in position for a relay. There wasn't anyone on the team that I disliked. That's rare. I am a pretty tough judge of people sometimes. If I don't like someone, I won't get in an argument with him. I'll stay away from him.

Martin (second row, third player from l) played Little League baseball three years for the Shamrocks.

I believe I remember every game I pitched. I remember a lot of games that I didn't pitch. There are some games that are completely out of my memory. It all came together in 1959 when I went 7-0 with three shutouts and a no-hitter against New Rochelle.

I knew on our team I was going to pitch every other game. Games were spaced out that way. By today's standards it would be over pitching. But everybody did it back then. Most high school teams, when we played, had two pitchers and a third guy who got in there.

In my sophomore and junior years I played a tremendous amount of summer ball. When you played summer ball then, you were really playing against All Stars from all over Westchester County. When we played the Yonkers Chippewa's, we played against players from all the schools in Yonkers. I'm not saying that I was fantastic. I had confidence.

I have to say that I was a pitcher and not a thrower. Pitching to me is the greatest thing in sports. You have control, and I'm not talking about wildness. You are in a thinking man's position. That is especially true when you play people you don't know.

In the major leagues they watch films and know what batters can do. At the high school level, and at the summer level, you have to make that judgment as you go along. I learned that very early in Little League and Pony League, especially in Little League, which was the most challenging because the mound was close.

You could get someone who throws very hard but can't get the ball over the plate. Little League pitchers mostly got the ball and just threw it. And most of those fellows never played in high school. Once players got to high school the pitching mound moved back a little further. Hitters matured.

And just as in the major leagues, there is always somebody who can hit that fast ball. No matter how fast someone throws it, there are going to be a couple of guys who can get around on it.

My thought was to keep the ball low. I wanted them to hit the ball on the ground. If it worked you had a good shot. I had to mix speeds. I don't care what you are doing; if you keep throwing the same speed, you are going to get hit.

Even today if you look in the majors, if someone throws the ball up and in, that hitter knows probably the next pitch is going to be a curve outside. I don't care if they know it or not. They are going to back off. The brain is saying, "Stupid, don't get hit by the ball."

I never tried to hit anybody in the head. But I did throw inside. The pitcher has a tremendous advantage if he does it right. That was my approach. Don't give anybody anything. It doesn't mean you can't walk anybody. You don't want to give a good hitter a good pitch. If he walks, he walks.

Looking back, the recreation programs were something special in Mount Vernon, not only for baseball, but basketball as well. I still talk to my sons about the Mount Vernon recreation leagues.

Eddie Martin: "My father and I caught a lot whenever he could. He was quite an athlete but not a baseball player."

Somebody had to organize the teams. Somebody had to get birth certificates and fill out forms and get permits to practice. I'm sure many of us had to do just that. It was a good experience. It taught me about responsibility and how to deal with older people who worked at City Hall where we got the permits.

Recreation games were also much looser. We organized everything ourselves. We made the batting order, assigned positions in basketball. That is missing today. It is sad when I go by a baseball field and see a bunch of kids in great uniforms. They look like they are totally bored. Maybe I'm wrong. We all know about the pressure parents put on kids. I saw a little of this in my own Little League career. But there was none of this when we played recreation ball in Mount Vernon.

In some ways I had kind of the best of both worlds growing up in Mount Vernon. A lot of my friends in Traphagen were Jewish. I wasn't. I had friends all over the place. On Rosh Hashanah and Yom Kippur, my friends Duffy, Scagnelli, Fusco, and I had a holiday. I knew kids who lived on the south side of Mount Vernon that my friends from Traphagen didn't know. Other than Mike Richman, most the kids from Traphagen went to summer camp.

A lot of my relatives lived on the south side of the city. I knew players from Little League who lived there. Most of the players came from Mount Vernon's south side and west side. The thought of crime or somebody beating you up was absent. That didn't exist, unless you were looking for trouble. You minded your business, played ball, went to the movies. It was a great place to grow up.

After high school, I played baseball for only two months more. The last game I played was at Memorial Field against an All Star team of soon-to-be Dodger rookies. It was a nice way to go out. It was a fund raiser for the 1960 US Olympic Team.

The guys we played against weren't professionals, but they were good. Memorial Field was packed. We used three pitchers. I started and threw three innings and did well. Shortly after that I couldn't throw a ball. I don't know exactly what happened.

I did pitch a lot that year both in high school and summer ball. That was the last baseball game I played. I started coaching with my friend Freddie O'Connor in the Mount Vernon Pony League in the late 1960s and early 1970s. I didn't pick up a ball until then. It hurt too much. I was able to throw batting practice.

In 1974, when my oldest son Ed went into the junior minor league in Mount Vernon, I became a coach and stayed with it until my two oldest boys finished. I liked coaching. It is a different experience. I got more frustrated coaching than playing. When my youngest son played, I coached again Bronxville in the Little Giants League. This was a completely different experience than coaching in Mount Vernon. It was much more low key. It was like recreation baseball in Mount Vernon. There weren't any standings. They kept score at the third and fourth grade level. The coaches would pitch to their own kids. So we didn't have a lot of walks. I got to like that approach.

I had planned to go to Fordham University and play baseball there. My arm injury put me back. I'm not sure of the sequence. I did not do well at all in high school through nobody's fault but my own. I was doing other things, not caring. I didn't do the work I should have done.

I actually did not graduate with my class in high school. It was another wakeup call. In some ways, it was a good wakeup call. It hurt like hell then. I failed the Latin regents. So I didn't have the language requirements to graduate. I had to make it up in the summer. But it was a wakeup call because here it was three weeks before when our principal Dr. Spalding was praising my name at an outdoor assembly because of baseball. I went to see him and asked him if something could be done about graduation. I didn't get anywhere with him. So it was lesson. All these things I believe are a help to you in the long run.

I remember working for a man, Joe Kahn, who was not quite old enough to be my father but certainly acted as a real big brother. He owned the local luncheonette in Chester Heights where I started working as a 13 year old. He eventually sold the store and opened a toy store in Elmsford. I went to work for him there.

I learned more about business in two years from Joe Kahn than I did from most of my college courses. He let me do almost everything. He went to California and I ran the store for him. I ordered for him. He could say things to me that my father couldn't say. I would shut off my father and my father would say, "Eddie what are you doing this for? What are you an idiot?"

I think those relationships, like being an apprentice to someone who is older than you, but will listen to you, works. I'm a big supporter of small businesses, not only for the businessman's sake, but for what someone can learn from that. You're doing everything in business. You're not an accountant. You're not a salesman. You're not a finance guy. As Joe Kahn often said, "Eddie, in small business retail you're in the infantry. Everybody is shooting at you."

Martin played shortstop between starts and led A.B. Davis in at bats, runs, and triples.

At Fordham University I majored in accounting. For whatever reason, I found that it worked for me. After graduating, I went to work for one of the then big eight accounting firms, Ernst & Ernst, Ernst & Young now. It was a great experience, but I left because the working hours were intolerable and if I stayed, I wasn't going to see my kids at all. I went to Iona to see if they had an accounting position, which they didn't. They had something called an accounting lab. That introduced me to teaching without too much of the responsibility. I didn't give out grades. I helped students. I did that for a year and then someone left, and I became full time teacher and eventually served as chairman of the accounting department. I was at Iona for 25 years beginning in 1971.

Since 1974 I have been president and director of the Hartsdale Pet Cemetery, a cemetery that my family has had a long association with. My father was a master engraver who, for more than four decades, designed and created most of the cemetery's monuments. My wife, Virginia, and I have three sons, Ed and Brian, who are part of the cemetery's full-time staff, while our third son Dan is a teacher in the Bronxville school district.

2 *Lenny Henderson*

When you talk about that '59 championship team, you have to talk about discipline, roll playing, teamwork, and a strong desire to win. Everybody tried to do their job. No one tried to do it all.

We had good pitching. Eddie Martin, Ernie Motta, and Bob Puccillo did their job. They won twelve of our fifteen games.

We had pretty talented guys. No one was so unusually overpowering that you would look to them for the answer. If you check the numbers from the games we played, it was obvious that we didn't blow anybody out regularly. It was always a tight game. That meant we had to have pretty good defensive skills. We didn't make a lot of errors.

We did what it took to win. We clawed our way to a lot of wins. If it was a one run game, we managed to get on base, steal second, move it around, and score somehow. It never was Teddy Cardasis having two home runs or Tommy Ambrosino, who was a clutch hitter, doing it all. These guys performed in and out regularly. But on a different day, somebody else would come through for us.

You have to go deep with Tony Cioppa. He was the tough guy on the team. He was the glue. He hit the ball real well. He was quite an athlete. Eddie Martin, you could depend on him. He was solid as a rock. Nicky Giordano had enormous talent. He may have been the best hitter outside of Ambrosino.

Lenny Henderson: "When you talk about that '59 team, you have to talk about discipline, roll playing, teamwork, and a strong desire to win."

I remember I was involved in two 1-0 wins. Against Commerce High School after Tony Cioppa walked and was balked to second base in the bottom of the fourth inning, I doubled him home for our only run of the game.

Almost the same thing happened two games later when Eddie Martin no-hit New Rochelle, 1-0. After I walked to open the bottom of the third, Cioppa drove me home with a double. How is that for coincidence?

When I first began playing baseball, I was a left fielder. But I played a lot of right field on our high school team. Then I ended up playing center field in college.

Back then I was quicker than I was fast. I probably had the

fastest first five or six steps. A fellow we went to school with who had real speed was Bobby Ross. Another fellow who could run was Alan Panoff; he played football with us.

You know baseball is really more scientific than most people realize. When you steal bases, it is really more technique than speed. But if you don't have any speed, you're in trouble. It's really all about timing and anticipation.

From the time I was a youngster I could read the pitchers real well. One of our high school coaches, Sully Mott, would say:

"Len, don't start running on your heels. Run on the ball of your feet." I had a tendency to run on my heels, which didn't enhance my speed.

At one time, while I was at Howard University, I was even leading the nation in stolen bases. I had a great sophomore year at Howard. I was captain of the team there for two years.

The great thing about that Howard team, and athletics in general, is that we truly were student athletes. Howard never gave away scholarships then. They gave away work grants. I think I may have had a grant for working in the gym and got paid for that.

Many of the fellows I played ball with there generally ended up as doctors, lawyers, and businessmen. Their primary focus was on academics and not sports.

But coming back to our high school team, if you ask me what I remember about that season, I'd have to say it was the bus rides and the songs we sang. It was a lot of fun.

I was the only black on the baseball team. Racism wasn't an issue when we played together in high school. I could say very clearly that the obvious racism wasn't there per se, particularly at the age when we played together. There is no doubt in my mind that kids were influenced by their parents about how we thought about other folks.

I think folks accepted people for what they were, and we were very aware that there were some differences. That's the way it was. No one thought any differently. Since then we've come a long way. But in relation to the team, though I may have represented the only black person on the team, it wasn't about color and religion. No one took a nose count of how many Catholics or Jews or Protestants were on that team. That's what made the team because of the relative unselfishness of team members and the many deep friendships.

Lenny Henderson: "He could run. I remember him stealing a lot of bases."

Lenny Fredriksen, who played football for us in high school, in my mind, has always been one of my best friends, and I've know him since pre-kindergarten. He's white. I grew up with Tony Cioppa, Eddie Lundquist, and all the guys who went to Robert Fulton Elementary School. Robert Fulton was nearly all white. They were my buddies. I really didn't really get the differentiation between races until I hit junior high school, which was Washington Junior High School.

Looking back, I have to say that I was born into Mount Vernon. I actually was born in Mount Pleasant, NY. The best I can remember is that I lived in a house at 26 Union Avenue in Mount Vernon that my dad, Allierson, bought in 1946. There's a lot of history in that house where I grew up. It's located about three houses down from the post office whose front is on First Avenue. That's where I started my formative years playing baseball.

I had three brothers, two older and one younger. The older ones were most influential. I remember there was a big wall near the post office. That's where I learned to play stickball. We drew a box on the wall that represented home plate. Guys like Cioppa, Fredriksen, and the Rowson brothers played there.

Henderson (front row, third from l) played for the Indians in the Mount Vernon Little League with high school teammate Teddy Cardasis (back row, fourth from r).

The Rowson brothers were great athletes and went to Edison Tech. The Henderson family and the Rowson family grew up together. The Rowsons lived two houses away. Interestingly, the Rowson brothers ended up as one of my first clients when I went into the insurance business back in 1967. They specialized in asphalt construction work and built playgrounds and driveways.

When I was very young we all played in the street on Union Avenue, against the wall. At Robert Fulton Elementary School our ball field became cement and dirt.

That's where I met Tony Cioppa for the first time. His dad and uncle owned a candy store on the corner of Union Avenue and Third Street called Cioppa's Stationery Store where you could sit down and have a soda or buy a candy bar. Tony and his cousin Billy worked there. Since Tony and I are the same age, I met him in Robert Fulton's kindergarten, or first grade, for sure.

We played football early on. We used to challenge the guys from Graham School and have some real wars with Dave Cromwell and Frank Cuomo from elementary school through junior high school. That's where I met my lifelong friend, Lenny Fredriksen.

My dad, Allierson Henderson Sr., was a Baptist minister at the Unity Baptist Church in Mount Vernon on Fifth Street and Sanford Boulevard. Now the church is located on First Avenue and Second Street.

He also was a politician. He became the first African American elected official in Westchester County when he was elected to the Board of Education in Mount Vernon in the 1950s. My mother, Lucelia Henderson, was a housewife.

How my dad got into real estate is an interesting story. At one time, he was president of the NAACP for Westchester County. Carl Farber, a white fellow, had a son, Carl Farber Jr., who wanted to go to Howard University, which had been exclusively a college for African Americans. For whatever reason, Carl Jr. wanted to go Howard. Carl Sr. approached my father because they were friends and said,

"Al, my son wants to go to Howard. Would you intercede to see if it could be done?"

My dad went to Washington DC and met with the then president of Howard University Mordecai Johnson. The next thing you know my dad calls Carl Sr. and says:

"Your son is now in Howard."

Well, Carl Sr. was so pleased he says to my father, "Al, you need to get into the real estate business."

Carl taught my father all about the real estate business. He became a real estate broker and eventually grew his real estate business into one of the largest African American real estate companies in Westchester County.

That's how I met Dave Cromwell, another great athlete at A.B. Davis. My dad sold Dave's parents their home near Graham School. In fact, my dad probably was responsible during that time for selling homes to most upward mobile African Americans who were moving into Mount Vernon.

A lot of folks anticipated that whatever I was going to do in life, I would come back and stay in Mount Vernon. All my brothers and I have college degrees and post graduate degrees but that was the inculcation of, quite frankly, my father and being raised in Mount Vernon.

I can remember my father buying me my first baseball mitt. That cost him $9.95. That was a lot of money back then. He bought it on Fourth Avenue. The reason he bought it was because I didn't make the Little League team the first time I tried out. I was assigned to a minor league club.

That team was called the Unicorns, and we practiced around Devonia Avenue near Pennington School in the north side of Mount Vernon. It seemed like a long way from my home on Union Avenue. But it really wasn't that far.

I don't know why I didn't make the Little League the first year. It might have been because I didn't make it to the tryouts. I ended up on the Unicorns and Teddy Cardasis, our high school teammate, was on it with me.

The next year we tried out for the Little League, and I ended up on the Indians. The Indians' coach was a chap named Steve Acunto, one of the foremost boxing instructors in the world. He was in ring demonstrations with the likes of Muhammad Ali, Rocky Marciano, and Willie Pep. He was inducted into the World Boxing Hall of Fame.

The Indians didn't have much fire power in the beginning. That's when I met our high school teammates Eddie Martin who played with the Shamrocks and also Ernie Motta. Ernie was legendary in Little League. Back then, Ernie had a big curve ball. Neil Arena also played with us. He was quite a baseball player.

I played left field more than anything else. Sometimes I'd play center. On our high school team I played right field because Nick Giordano played left. He was in the Little League too. John Fortier played with us also in Little League.

Growing up I never met a lot of the fellows on our high school baseball team like Bruce Fabricant and Steve Matthews who lived on the north side of Mount Vernon. I first met them when I was in junior high school and a bench warmer on our basketball team that played against Graham, Nichols, and Traphagen.

We also had a flag league amongst the junior high schools where I played football with many of our high school baseball teammates. What I could sense is that we could have had one heck of a football team if there was one high school in Mount Vernon and not two. Many of the outstanding junior high school kids went to Edison Tech. Had they gone to A.B. Davis that would have given us the added depth and beef to compete with New Rochelle and White Plains.

Henderson led the Howard University Bisons in 1962 with a .370 batting average and stolen bases.

After high school I graduated from Howard University in Washington D.C. and then finished law school. I was recruited by Metropolitan Life Insurance but only worked for Met Life for one year because of an ROTC military commitment. I spent 3½ years in the Air Force at Mountain Home Air Force Base in Idaho and took the bar examination there and became the first black to pass the Idaho bar.

While I have a law degree, I've never practiced law. I retired early after spending 23 years with Metropolitan Life Insurance, working primarily in Washington DC and Dayton, Ohio. I have been involved in the insurance business in the Bahamas, shuttling between the Bahamas and Columbia, Maryland.

I have been married since 1967 and have two daughters, one a doctor in the Washington DC area, the other daughter, a graduate of the University of Michigan, who attended Howard University law school for a while. There is also a grandson in the family.

3 *Tommy Ambrosino*

I used to catch with my mother even before I played in the Little League. My mother, Margaret, had a catcher's mitt, and we'd throw to each other in our driveway at 23 North Tenth Avenue. She was quite athletic. She was the one who helped me become a pitcher.

You see, my dad, Joseph, had his own business. He sold potato chips, pretzels, and candies to grocery stores. He was always working six days a week. My parents and younger sister, Nancy, and I lived in a private house, five doors down from the North Side Boys Club.

My cousin, Vincent Carosella, lived around the corner, and we played ball together all the time. He was a little older than me. We played in the street and the backyard. I remember my father and uncle sometimes taking us to Longfellow School and Hutchinson Field to play ball on Saturdays and Sundays when there weren't Little League games.

I also remember a gentleman, Dr. Joseph Mangano, who lived right next door to us. That was long before he became a doctor. When he was in college, we had catches in the driveway that separated our houses. About that time my father bought me my first glove at Tom Godfrey's sports store on the corner of Gramatan and Prospect Avenues.

I forget how old I was when I tried out for Little League. My grandfather, who was always working in his grocery store, showed up for the first day of tryouts. I remember I was in the outfield and a ball was hit to me. It took a bad bounce and smacked me right in the nose, breaking my nose. I started bleeding and went down to the ground. My father and coaches ran out to see how I was doing.

"Well, he can come back next week and try out again," one of the coaches said to my father. "He'll be ready in ten minutes," my father replied. Ten minutes later I was back in the outfield again. They wanted to see if I'd be ball shy. I wasn't. I made the team.

Tommy Ambrosino: "He had real good hand-to-eye coordination and could hit to all fields."

I'll tell you, I had an interesting Little League career. I probably was one of the only kids ever traded in the Mount Vernon Little League. My cousin Vincent and a friend, Dickie Morgenthau, were also traded with me. The three of us played for the Indians when Steve Acunto was the manager and Joseph Tripodi was the assistant coach.

The manager hardly played us even though we went to every practice. We never missed one. When I finally got into a game, the manager had me bunting. Then I was taken out. Vincent, Dickie and I were annoyed and said, "Why bother. He's not playing us. He's not giving us a chance."

We told our fathers that we were going to quit. So our fathers went to Joe Tripodi, who they knew, and told him that we were getting down. We were down even though we went to all the practices. Our fathers told him that Steve Acunto wasn't giving us a chance. Tripodi told our dads to speak to us and tell us to hang in. But he didn't want our dads to tell us that he was starting his own team the following year. So that spring Tripodi took over a team called The Pirates. Vincent, Dickie and I were probably the only kids in the Mount Vernon Little League who were traded from one team to another. The best is that the same year we were traded we beat the Indians in the playoff and won a championship. Steve Acunto, to this day, has never spoken to assistant coach Joseph Tripodi.

That was quite a team. Johnny Tripodi played second base. Frankie Cuomo was at third. Eddie Lombardi, who later was in the New York Mets organization, was in center field. John Forkell caught. I played leftfield. And Pat Tucci was in right. I think Paul LoGuercio pitched.

I remember another kid who played the outfield. He couldn't catch a fly ball if it had honey on it. It was a shame because I recall his parents used to push him. You see, in the Little League everybody had to play. But I don't remember ever seeing him with a baseball glove on his hand. He would apologize to us every time he played. He'd be in the outfield, and the batter would hit a fly ball to him, and we'd lose the game. But I remember that he was so intelligent. I think he even tied a US chess champion when he was the age of a Little Leaguer. The kid didn't have television or a radio in his house, just books. Who knows what he is today. I wonder where his career took him.

I remember my mother and father came to those night games at Longfellow School, off South Fifth Avenue, and at Baker Field on California Road. The games began at 5:30 and 6:00 pm. The kids loved those games. You see, my father sold Treat Potato Chips. He had a truck. He'd drive up with his truck and give out small bags of potato chips at all the practices and games. They were called nickel bags then. You can't use that term anymore because of drugs. But the kids on the team really enjoyed those potato chips. Little things like that kids remember.

I'll tell you, we really had a good time playing in high school. We were all nice guys. We were a team, not just a bunch of guys out for themselves. When someone was down, another guy would pick him up. Everybody was trying to win. It wasn't just me, me, and me. That was the best thing about that team. We were together. And we sure had laughs on those bus rides. I remember when someone stole my sandwiches after a game. I'd bring a sandwich to away games because I was hungry on the long ride home. Somebody saw me eating and one day they went into my bag and stole my sandwich.

In that championship season I think I hit .371. That helped me get honorable mention for All County. I wasn't a home run hitter. I'd hit singles and doubles and occasionally a triple. I was a little, short, fat guy at the time. And I wasn't fast. I was a pretty good bunter. I remember one time Frankie Fiore was on third base. I gave him the squeeze sign myself and bunted him home. The sign didn't come from our coach. That's the way we played ball then.

I remember the first game of that season when I sat out against Nyack. I also sat later on because I missed practice. The next game I pinched hit and doubled over the centerfielder's head. I had some good days. I remember one game going 3-4. I was a pretty decent hitter, a line-drive and gap hitter basically. I started off playing third base and then moved over to first. I even pitched a little. That was in our senior year.

I remember Coach Sywetz asking me to throw the shot in gym one day. But wouldn't you know it, that afternoon he tells me that I'm pitching. So I start throwing what I think are fastballs. The pitches are crossing the plate at maybe 40 miles per hour. My arm was gone from throwing the shot.

Let me tell you about some of the players on that team. I knew Eddie Martin and his mother and father and sister since Little League. His mom and dad were very instrumental in the program. I think his mother was secretary treasurer for quite a few years. We played against each other when he was on the Shamrocks and also later again when we were in the Pony League. He was a good pitcher and a nice guy. I knew him later on in Bronxville when I worked there.

Ambrosino led A.B. Davis in hitting with a .379 average and was named Honorable Mention All Westchester County.

Tommy Ambrosino: "He was one of those guys who came on and was better as a junior than as a sophomore."

Then there's Teddy Cardasis. He's always been a good friend. I knew his parents who were friends with my mother and father. He was some ball player. I remember he got hurt and couldn't bat righty. He then batted lefty and did just as good job as when he batted right-handed. He had some arm. He was very funny when he wanted to be.

Lenny Henderson could run. I remember him stealing a lot of bases. I understand when he went to college at Howard University he played ball there and for a while was leading the country in stolen bases. Bruce Fabricant at second base was always spunky. He was like the little engine that couldn't, but he did. He wasn't afraid of getting hurt and knocked down on a double play ball. Neil Arena also was a good ballplayer. He was a little flashy in the pants. I still see him occasionally. I saw him at

Mount Vernon Day in Florida last year.

You know I don't remember much about Mike Abrams. I know he was in the class ahead of us. Tony Cioppa and I played against each other going back to our Little League days. He was a nice guy, not flashy, kind of laid back and never too loud. He was a good player, someone you could rely on. Another solid ball player was Nicky Giordano. He was also very quiet and a good friend. We played together for The Cotts and won a championship.

Looking back, Mount Vernon was a good sports town when I was a kid. I was born and lived there until I married. There were so many leagues to play in when we grew up. There was Little League, Pony League and then a PAL League. I remember Dorothy Bourne, who sponsored the Paramounts. You had to picture this lady. She was about 5-feet 8-inches tall and weighed about 220. She wore big, round, flashy hats like you'd see in old movies on television. She came to the games but was dressed like she was going to a dance.

My entire family grew up and lived in Mount Vernon, on both my mother's and father's side. After graduation, I worked for Borden's Milk Company for a while as a home delivery man. Then I went into the Marine Corps Reserves and was shipped to Parris Island in South Carolina for six months. I spent five years in the reserves. After I got out, I found a job at the Borden's plant on Washington and Fulton streets in Mount Vernon. You might remember the building with the big metal milk container on top. That's where I was introduced to my wife, Lucille, who was working in the office. We've been married 45 years.

Lucille and I moved to Bronx River Road in Yonkers when we got married and had a son, Joseph. We needed more room so we moved to my mother's two-family house on North Tenth Avenue where we stayed for 10 years. In the meantime, we had two girls, Nancy and Jennifer. Then we bought a house in Scarsdale and lived there for 27 years while the kids went to Scarsdale schools.

Coach Bill Sywetz.

I was a cop in Mount Vernon from 1968 to 1969 and took the test for towns and villages in Westchester County. I came out tenth on the county list and was appointed to the Village of Bronxville's Police Department. From there I was promoted to sergeant and retired as a lieutenant after 37 years of service.

When I was working as a patrolman in Bronxville in1980, I delivered a baby boy in a house in Bronxville when a pregnant woman called the department. She had to get to the hospital as quickly as she could. I was the first policeman ever to deliver a baby in the Bronxville Police Department. The doctor even had me come to the hospital after the delivery and co-sign the boy's birth certificate. We were invited to his christening.

Lucille and I are now living in Naples, Florida. And wouldn't you know it, my cousin Vincent lives only about 15 miles from me. We're still close, almost like brothers. It's North Tenth Avenue all over again.

4 Nick Giordano

Ask Nick Giordano what catch was the most talked about he ever made.

No contest. The catch I made on Pete Peadmont of New Rochelle when Eddie Martin threw his no hitter.

We were leading 2-0 in the bottom of the fourth inning at Hutchinson Field. Peadmont was built like and looked like Mickey Mantle at the plate. He batted right-handed. I remember him hitting the ball a mile high. As soon as I picked it up in the sky, I knew I had to get to the foul line in left field. I turned and ran with my back to the plate. I jumped over a telephone pole that was lying on the ground that separated a car path and the outfield. I timed it perfectly. I was waiting for the ball to drop down into my glove.

Was it the greatest catch I ever made? Most of my teammates thought it was the greatest catch of the season. I don't think so. I made two nice catches in that New Rochelle game: the one everyone remembers and one they don't.

Peadmont hit a line drive down the left field line that was towards Pelham Field. I got a great jump on the ball. I just ran a short distance, leaped, and caught it in my webbing. That ball would have been gone along with Eddie's no-hitter if I hadn't caught it. That was a much harder catch. It was a slam, bam, bang play. People didn't realize how difficult a catch it was because I didn't have time to run and catch the ball. It happened so fast.

Nick Giordano: "He had enormous talent and may have been the best hitter outside of Tom Ambrosino."

Good defensive plays were what our team was all about in 1959. It was good defense without much hitting. When Eddie threw his no-hitter, he had only three strikeouts. He had to have a good defense behind him to do what he did. A man who pitches a no-hitter with only three strikeouts says a lot for his defense behind him. There were a lot of ground balls and fly balls that game and all season long.

That year we all got along with each other. Everybody pretty much knew one another since most of us were in the same grade. We were juniors and went up the ladder together playing Little League and Pony League ball. Teddy Cardasis and I were friends since the seventh grade at Nichols Junior High School. We've been great friends ever since and stay in touch with each other. Teddy had the most natural instincts of anyone I ever knew. He reminded me of Ted Williams at bat. I used to help him wrist curl 400 pounds. Two of us had to help put the weights in his hands. He had such powerful wrists. That would help him hit the ball a country mile. He was a skinny kid.

Mike Abrams was a good hitter. So was Tommy Ambrosino who shared third base with Mike in the beginning of the season. Tommy led the team in hitting. Neil Arena was a year ahead of us and was a utility infielder who played short and second. Tony

Cioppa was a good athlete. He caught for us. He's the reason why we didn't win much in our senior year. He didn't play that year. Bruce Fabricant was steady Eddie at second base. He reminded me of Bobby Richardson. He moved quite a few runners along with timely sacrifices and was reliable in the field. Lenny Henderson was the bunter and could run like a deer. He used to get on base a lot. He wasn't a power hitter.

Eddie Martin did a great job of pitching because of his control. He really mixed up his pitches. Through the years, I played a lot against Ernie Motta. He was on the Eagles in the Little League. We both made the All Star teams together in Little League and Pony League. We were always adversaries until we got to high school. He was pretty good. He used to throw a low ball, a sinker. Frank Fiore was a utility infielder. He was a quiet guy and never complained if he didn't play. Steve Matthews was another sub who played first base occasionally. I remember his father, Mr. Matthews, came to all the games. I'll never forget him. He was a big fan. John Fortier played some outfield and Bob Puccillo pitched and won two key games for us that season.

We had different lineups in most of our games. But if you look it up, you'll see that I started in left field in all 16 games. I competed against Richard Giloth, Fortier, Cardasis, and Henderson for an outfield spot. Teddy, Lenny and I won the positions. Once the season began, I got hits in our first three games. The one game I do remember was when we played and beat White Plains 5-2. In the fifth inning I doubled to drive in Eddie Martin and Tony Cioppa. I think I had five putouts in left field that game.

After that high school season we formed a team called The Hilltoppers from the guys on our championship team. We played in a recreation league against teams from different towns like Port Chester and Rye. I remember my father got sick with Parkinson's disease when I was 14 and wasn't very mobile. My brother took him to one of our Hilltoppers games in Port Chester where we lost 2-1.

I kept playing ball after graduating from A.B. Davis. I played

American Legion hardball and fast-pitch softball at Hutchinson Field. We won a championship playing softball for Mount Carmel. Ralph Fatigate pitched and Ralph Carbone and I were the top hitters. Ralph was amazing. He was an older guy, but he sure could hit.

Giordano (bottom row, second from r) pitched and played the outfield for the Cotts All Stars in the Mount Vernon Pony League.

I didn't pitch when I was older, but in the lower grades I pitched a great deal. In the Pony League, playing for the Cotts, I remember throwing a one-hitter against The Vets. I also remember Coach Sywetz, in my junior year of high school, asking me to become a pitcher. "If I pitch and when I don't pitch, can I play the outfield?" I replied." "No," he said. "Then I'm going to compete for a spot in the outfield." I'd rather play all time than sit on the bench waiting to pitch. Then the next year, my senior year, I asked him, "If you want me to pitch, I'll pitch." I think he was a little upset and said, "I don't need you this year."

Mount Vernon was a good place to grow up. I couldn't ask for a better place what with all those ball fields around me. I was born in Mount Vernon Hospital. We lived across the street from Nichols Junior High School at 442 North High Street in a four-family house. I was lucky to be near three ball fields right across the street from our house.

My father, Michael Angelo Giordano, was a stone mason who learned his trade in Italy. He came to the United States with the Italian Navy in World War I. When the war was over, he docked in Maryland and jumped ship and settled in Mount Vernon. He was a man who couldn't speak the English language and had no money. He ended up starting his own family here and left his other family behind in Italy. He could never go back because he was absent without leave from the service. He married my mother, Marie, and they raised three children, my brother, Joe, who is eight years older than I, and my sister, Teresa, who is six years older.

Joe helped got me interested in baseball. When I was a kid he showed me how to play ball. He had an old glove, probably something like Phil Rizzuto used when he was a kid. Little lumps of fingers covered his hand. When I made the Little League he bought me a Spalding glove at Tom Godfrey's.

We played catch all the time. We had the pick of three ball fields: the Nichols playground; A.B. Davis High School middle field between Nichols and Davis; and the high school.

As I got older, I started playing with Tony Moretti, Pete Pucillo, Tom Girardi, John Girardi, Vinny Rocco, and Basil Champion in the neighborhood. We had a softball team that competed against other playground clubs from Hartley Park, Brush Park, and Howard Street, We must have been pretty good since we won the Mount Vernon Recreation Department championship several times.

I remember playing ball from morning 'til night. My mother would yell out the window and call me home for supper. She had quite a pair of lungs. I could hear her up all the way up the street yelling, "Come and eat." She screamed that to get us home.

Nick Giordano: "I remember his incredible catch over the logs in left field."

We played all types of ball. There were handball courts behind Nichols where we played ball. We would take a chalk and mark a box on the wall. I'd play against another kid and we'd throw a tennis ball. If it hit the box, it was a strike. We had different markers for a single, double, triple and home run.

I really don't remember trying out for the Little League. I remember I was ten years old. When you're ten, your coordination is way behind eleven-and twelve-year-olds. So I sat on the bench and watched most of the games. I played for the Peacocks, and Joe Moccio was my coach for one year, and then Mr. Mangone managed another year. Donnie Ross was our catcher, and I pitched and played the outfield. Donnie was an excellent ballplayer. He actually lived in the Bronx over the line from Mount Vernon. Tom Mangone and Tommy Ambrosino were also on the team. When Tommy wasn't batting third or fifth in the lineup, then I would be in those spots. Bottom line, as a 10-year-old, I didn't get a hit and sat on the bench. As an 11-year-old, I played and started in the outfield and also pitched. As a 12-year-old I was an all star.

After all those years growing up and living in Mount Vernon, who would have thought I'd end up in Durham, Connecticut? I was living in Mount Vernon when I got married at 36 in 1979. My wife is from Massachusetts. Our son, Michael, was six months old when we moved to Connecticut in 1982 because I was working in Woodbridge and driving 60 miles one way. So we moved to Connecticut into a garden apartment. I went to the Durham Fair, the largest agricultural fair in Connecticut after they closed The Danbury Fair, and fell in love with the town and bought a house in Durham.

Nick Giordano: "Good defensive plays were what our team was all about in 1959."

That's where I taught Michael how to field and hit. He was a pretty good ballplayer. I couldn't manage, so I coached his Little League team. I quickly found out the trouble with Little League in Durham was politics. The manager played favorites, his son's favorites, his relatives. It wasn't fair. It's a lot different living in the boondocks than Mount Vernon. You need a car to get anywhere, and there are only a few kids in the neighborhood. There really isn't any place to play. In Mount Vernon we walked everywhere. Sometimes, I'd go to Fleetwood and play basketball or to Pennington School and play there also.

For over 30 years I was a financial consultant before I retired. I had my own marketing company, Durham Marketing, with an office in Woodbridge and also in Oklahoma. I was legislated out of business because of the 1986 tax law that did away with the write-off on the private placements I did. I then worked for Merrill Lynch for a while, and, for the last 10 years, I have been a financial consultant in the banking industry.

Living up here in Durham, I'm a big Connecticut Huskies basketball fan. My two kids graduated from UConn. I follow the women's team more than the men's team. Do you remember Jennifer Rizzotti? From 1992 to 1996, she starred on the women's basketball team at UConn. She was the starting point guard on the Huskies first national championship team in 1995. She's currently the head women's basketball coach at the University of Hartford.

Jen was here in Durham at Coginchaug Regional High School not too long ago to present an award to an academic scholar. I saw her and said to my wife, "That woman has to be either the daughter of Tom Rizzotti or Phil Rizzotti from Mount Vernon. She has a head just like them."

My wife thought I was nuts. We then went to the table where Jen was signing autographs and I asked her, "What are Tom and Phil Rizzotti, the twins from Mount Vernon, to you?" She looked at me in amazement and said, "Tom's my father and Phil's my uncle." My wife turned to me and said, "You were right."

I had played on a recreation league football team with Tom and Phil for a year. Tom Rizzotti was a very determined guy. I'm sure that's where his daughter Jennifer got her determination. I remember he wanted to play fast pitch softball but really couldn't pitch. He worked at it. He practiced and became a good pitcher. His brother caught him.

5 *Tony Cioppa*

There's a great story about the first time I met Eddie Martin. We were in Little League playing against each other, and my coach put me in to catch. In fact, that was the first time I ever caught in a game. Eddie was on the other team. He comes up to bat and drives the ball between the outfielders and tries to stretch it into a home run.

As he rounds the bases and heads home everybody in the stands starts screaming at me, "Block the plate. Block the plate." He comes into home plate and I step on his leg with my spikes. He starts bleeding profusely.

The next thing I know I look in the stands and my mother and his mother are screaming at each other. They almost came to blows. That's how I met Eddie.

Jump ahead a couple of years, and now we're in high school. Eddie is the pitcher and I'm the catcher on our championship team. Even then, in my junior year, I was still like a virgin type of catcher. I didn't know everything about the position.

But I'll tell you one thing. Every time I put the mitt down, the ball went right into the mitt. No matter where I put the mitt, he put the ball in the right place. We would mix it up and go side to side on batters. They weren't getting around. It was a like a miracle. Wherever the mitt went, the ball landed there, curveballs, straight balls, you name it.

It was unbelievable how accurate he was. The break on his

curve was just perfect. It wasn't a big wrinkle. It was a snappy curve ball. They couldn't hit. They couldn't touch it. Then, when I moved outside, the same thing; they couldn't touch it.

I called the game for Eddie. He was a fast worker on the mound. It was one pitch after another; bing, bing, bing.

I caught all three of his shutouts that season. Catching the other guys seemed to be a struggle. It was a little harder for me. Our other key starter, Ernie Motta, was a little faster than Eddie. Ernie quite often would get into trouble. But he seemed to get out of most of it.

I caught 15 out of the 16 games we played. I didn't catch the last game of the season, a 12-3 win against our cross-town rival Edison Tech. The reason why I wasn't behind the plate in that game is because I think our coach thought I was too friendly with the other side. You see, I had quite a few friends playing for Edison.

I had a pretty good season catching. For some reason my arm strength was stronger during my junior year. Wherever I threw the ball, it was right on target. Not too many runners ran on me. We had a lot of caught stealing. I remember throwing down to Martin who played shortstop when he wasn't pitching and to Neil Arena and Bruce Fabricant, our second basemen.

I enjoyed hitting and batted .325 that season mostly from the three and fourth spots in the batting order. I didn't hit a lot of line drives. I remember hitting long high fly balls that season and throughout my baseball career. The first time I saw a curve ball in high school was a sophomore; it seemed to look like the size of a saucer up there. I hit it into the creek out beyond left field at Hutchinson Field for a home run.

I guess the biggest hit I had in our championship season was the 350-foot double I had against New Rochelle when Eddie threw his 1-0 no hitter. Lenny Henderson came around from first to score. That was the type of ball I hit. They were big long fly balls. I had a lot of strength that year at bat.

I actually tried to study and copy the way Mickey Mantle

would hit. The way he hit left handed was different than the way he hit right handed. I would try to emulate him as right handed batter. I tried to use my forearm muscles like Mickey. He would tense up and relax, tense up and relax. I did the same thing. All of a sudden that season, the ball seemed to jump off my bat. It would shock me sometimes how far the ball would go.

Tony Cioppa, left, brother Tom, and sister Angela.

It was never about the coach that season. Quite often, we used have to tell the coach what to do. Everything we seemed to tell him worked out pretty good.

I remember Coach Sywetz at Washington Junior High School before he came to A.B. Davis. He was our gym teacher in junior high school. Once after school we were playing a basketball game. My cousin and I were on one team. We were considered the smart kids, and we were playing fellows who eventually would go to vocational high school.

We won the game, but right after it my cousin, Robert, tells Coach Sywetz that there are some kids out in the hallway who were going to beat me up. Coach Sywetz came out into the hallway and pinned several of them up against the wall. I'll never forget that.

From behind the plate that '59 season I had a pretty good perspective watching our team play ball. We played as a real team. There were individuals on the team who excelled in different ways.

We had that perfect combination. Someone would jump up and do the right thing. That's what happened. It was the combination of the first baseman making a good play, or a third baseman making a good play. We would always come up with a clutch hit at the right time.

Teddy Cardasis was a great player. He was a Ted Williams type of hitter. He had a great swing and an unbelievable outfield arm. He made All County honorable mention in the outfield that year. He also played football for us at A.B. Davis.

I'll tell you how he made the football team. We were out on the field behind the high school during gym class and I was throwing the ball around. I threw a *Hail Mary* pass, and up jumps Teddy who grabs the ball. The football coaches saw this. The next thing you know they made him an end on our high school team.

I also remember Steve Matthews. He played a little first base. He had a swing and a half but didn't make too much contact. We played a lot of football together, which I know was his better sport. Nicky Giordano and John Fortier were good outfielders. Frankie Fiore, Neil Arena, and Bruce Fabricant were in the infield. Any time I threw down to second base, their glove was right there. Neil was a good singer and a good shortstop. Tommy Ambrosino, at third base, made All County honorable mention.

Teddy Cardasis: "Teddy had the most natural instincts of anyone I ever knew."

I also played football for A.B. Davis. But baseball was always my favorite sport. I wanted to be a lineman, a guard. The coaches put me at fullback for some dopey reason. When I was playing guard, right next to me was Wendell Tyree who was our tackle. We were moving everybody out. Then the coach saw how I was doing this with my legs. He moved me to fullback. I didn't want to play that position because I knew I didn't have the speed.

My best game against Roosevelt High School in my junior year was when I got hurt. I couldn't play baseball in my senior year because my knee got whacked pretty good in that Roosevelt game. We had an off tackle play left and an off tackle play right. The play was going great until I was tackled hard around my knees.

I went to see Dr. Henry Carideo. Here's an interesting story. I believe Dr. Carideo was related to Frank Carideo who was the quarterback on Knute Rockne's last two Notre Dame teams that went 19-0. He is a member of the College Football Hall of Fame. Frank Carideo was born in Mount Vernon and went to Mount Vernon High School.

So who takes my place at fullback after I go down with the injury? Henry Carideo. He must have been Dr. Carideo's son.

That injury impacted my baseball career. In an early season baseball practice in my senior year, my father comes out and grabs me and says, "That's it. You're not playing sports anymore because of your knee." That's why I didn't play baseball in my senior year.

I was born in Mount Vernon and lived in an apartment house at Union Avenue and Third Street. We had a candy store there. At that time my father, Antonio, was in the Army. He was drafted near the end of World War II and was shipped to Amarillo, Texas.

I actually remember him coming home from the Army. My mother, Rosina, was giving me a bath when he walked in. The joke in the family was that he ended the war by getting drafted.

My dad worked in that candy store/luncheonette with his brother. My grandfather had owned the luncheonette. So my dad then ran the luncheonette with my uncle until my dad died when he was 53 years old.

I have a brother, Tom, and a sister, Angela. My sister and I are one year apart, and Tom is six years younger than me. I felt bad for him when he first went to A.B. Davis. It seems all the coaches wanted him to be a ballplayer like me. He loves baseball. In fact, he played a lot longer than I did after high school because he stayed in better shape than I did. He is now a school teacher in New Rochelle.

We had a garage in our backyard and would play stickball

against the garage. That's how I began playing baseball. In that same backyard our family would have parties, family get-togethers, and stuff like that. My uncles would throw a ball up in the air and make me catch it. That's how I learned to judge fly balls.

Tony Cioppa: "He wasn't flashy, kind of laid back, never too loud, and someone you could rely on."

In the neighborhood we had a bunch of Irish kids, the Deegan family, and we would play in the backyard. They would take my father's Knickerbocker beer off the porch sometimes. We also had a basketball net back there as well as a field in the Deegan's yard where we played baseball.

I remember playing a lot of stickball at Robert Fulton Elementary School with Lenny Henderson. There was a big field there. We used to play saloogie, a game of *keep away* that was popular in the 1950s. Two or more players simply took something from another kid and threw it back and forth, tormenting the kid while the kid tried desperately to get his property back. There was a lot of running and ball throwing.

We were outside there playing baseball morning 'til night. My mother quite often had to send people like my sister or my neighbors out to get me.

We had many friends who lived near the playground at Robert Fulton School. We would go to Lenny Fredriksen's or Carl Lugbauer's house for lunch and would learn about different nationalities. It was very interesting to be in a Swedish or Norwegian house and see and eat different foods.

I found my first glove down at Hutchinson Field. It was a real shortstop's glove. It was a good one. It was broken in and very flexible. That was the glove I used for a long time. My father used to buy me gloves, but they weren't the same as that first one.

I had an unfortunate incident with the Little League when I first tried out as a nine years old. I made the team, the Indians, and my father was happy about that. The coach, I think his name was Mr. Tripodi, then cut me from the team and replaced me with another kid who was older than me. That was politics. My father got mad and consequently would not let me play in the Little League until I was twelve when I made the Bears.

I could always hit and remember hitting quite a few home runs that year. We were sluggers and we won everything. I played shortstop, and I remember our teammate Ernie Motta was around playing in the Little League at that time. That's when I first met him.

I began catching when a coach saw that I had a strong arm. He tried to make me a pitcher but put me behind the plate. The first game I ever caught was when I spiked Eddie Martin. I caught the rest of my career.

I really liked catching because I was into the game all the time. I didn't have a chance to day dream. Once when I did play third base and was day dreaming, the coach hit a ball that ricocheted off my chest. He did it on purpose. He is the same guy who moved me to catcher.

Baseball always was my favorite sport growing up. Baseball is a sport that is blessed. It isn't a violent sport. It's a great game for boys and girls. Baseball is an ideal sport even if you want to be a score keeper or a fan. It is a gift.

You can play as an individual within a team concept. Baseball, basically an American sport, is a great gift to this country. I truly believe that God blessed us with this sport to keep our children out of trouble. It's the greatest sport there is because it is a team sport, and yet you are an individual within that team. You can excel all by yourself, and you can end up rooting for people who you never thought you would root for in your life, blacks, whites, Spanish.

Growing up we would watch the Yankees on television all the time. My father was a Giants fan. Maybe that is why he liked Knickerbocker beer. Knickerbocker was a Giants sponsor. One uncle was a Red Sox fan and another was a Dodgers fan. So we always were in competition.

When I was little we went to Giants games at the Polo Grounds because that was my dad's team. Later I went to the Dodgers games because a lady across the street was afraid to go by herself. So she used to take me with her. We would end up sitting in the middle of all these Giants fans while she would be cheering for the Dodgers.

I recall my father took me to the Giants games thinking I would help them win. You see, the Yankees would win whenever I went to the Yankees with the Con Edison kids from Mount Vernon. We would sit in the centerfield bleachers that were later blacked out to help hitters follow the ball. We would sit there for doubleheaders. I remember watching Gene Woodling hit an inside-the-park home run there. There were a lot more inside the park home runs at Yankee Stadium then because the field was so big.

I also remember watching the Red Sox's Jimmy Piersall get into a fight that turned into a near riot when the fans got on him. I was there with my son at the 1996 American League Championship Series when Jeffrey Maier reached over the wall and gave the New York Yankees' Derek Jeter a home run.

When we were young growing up there, Mount Vernon was a small town, only four square miles. There were times when we found ourselves on the other side of town at Pennington School or at the Traphagen playground. We used to be able to walk from home to A.B. Davis every day. We met people along the way. Sometimes we had a fight. No one really got hurt. It was a peaceful town basically.

Tony Cioppa, center: "I can still see the home run he smacked into the creek at Hutchinson Field as a sophomore."

Third Street was a great place to shop or to eat pizza, like at Johnny's Pizza located next to the Fanny Farmer candy store. There were ice cream stores all over the place. Anything you wanted was on Third Street. My father's store was on the Union and Third. There were delicatessens and luncheonettes all over. It was a great atmosphere.

After high school I played a lot of softball, very little hardball. I started working for the U.S. Post Office in Mount Vernon. The office was at Third Street, near Pape's Bowling Alley.

That's another reason why my father pulled me off of the team. The post office offered me a job in the summer time and when they got busy throughout the year. When I was in the U.S. Army National Guard for six years, I worked at the post office on weekends. They always had a job for me because my uncle knew the boss there. They liked me and eventually made a supervisor.

I wound up living in an apartment house at 101 Elwood Avenue with my wife, Mary Ellen, near Traphagen. We stayed there until 1972 and moved to our current home in Lincolndale in Somers. I never heard of Somers before that. But did you know that Somers was in line to be the site for the United Nations at one time? It would have been where the Pepsi Cola bottling headquarters is now located.

I became a supervisor in the postal service and commuted to Rockland County where I ran a facility in Monsey. I then became a postmaster in Armonk, New York, for five years and eventually retired. Mary Ellen and I have one child, a son Aaron. He has a daughter Rebecca Rose. Rebecca is the name of my wife's mother, and Rose was my mother's name.

I still wear the t-shirt Eddie Martin gave each of us. That's the one that says A.B. Davis on the front and WIAA champions on the sleeve. People still come up to me and say, "I know where that place is."

That shirt is a great way to start a conversation with people you never knew.

6 *Mike Abrams*

We were just a bunch of kids that enjoyed playing baseball for the sake of playing. There was a certain common bond. Even today when I meet certain people, we always seem to relate to that era of the 50s. The person who I was closest to was Richie Shapiro, one of our teammates. Until the day he died in 1998 at the age of 57 he was the closest and best of friends.

I had lost contact with him after high school until I moved to Rockland County. We lived around the corner from each other in New City. Richie and I would sit for hours reminiscing about our youth. It was a sense of security. We were insulated from the rest of the world. It was a very, very secure feeling. We talked a great deal about sports and growing up in Mount Vernon.

We had a common bond that existed ever since we were young and grew up in Mount Vernon. His wife, Barbara, lived around the corner from me, and we shared a lot of things growing up. When I remarried and moved to Rockland's New City, Richie and Barbara lived near us. At that moment, based upon our common bond, we rekindled our friendship.

The way we described our relationship was, "Not everyday was Saturday night." We could sit and talk. We knew each others warts and the good things, and bad things. It was a comforting relationship.

We talked about our high school teams and the championship team we both played on. During our run in that

'59 championship season, I missed playing in the first five games of my senior season because I had the chicken pox.

The year before, the baseball coach, Irv Halstead, said to me once, "Why don't you give up on baseball and play tennis." I was offended when he said that and went out and made the team as a senior.

We really didn't have stars on that championship team. I remember, as a junior, the baseball team was composed of guys who thought that they walked on water. They didn't win that many games. We didn't have anyone like that on our club. We just plugged along. We did what we had to do.

What I remember as a senior is that we did not have an overpowering club. Not that I want to put Eddie Martin in his place, but to this day I don't remember how Eddie won all of those games. He wasn't overpowering. I was amazed he was able to do what he did. He didn't throw the ball 100 miles per hour. We had a good defensive squad. We made the plays. We did what we had to do. We executed. We were consistent. That was the way it was. And Eddie, he got the job done.

In '59, things just started to come together. We were in the right place at the right time. We didn't have guys hitting tremendous home runs. Honestly, I don't remember all the details. But we had a nice bunch of guys.

We had Lenny Henderson on the team who was as quick as can be. There was Neil Arena. I always respected Neil because of his great basketball ability.

After I got out of college, Neil was refereeing high school basketball games in the county. There was a game in which one of my sons was playing against New Rochelle High School. I walked into the gym and who is there but Neil. He recognized me and we started talking. The game was delayed for ten minutes because we were just going on and on about the old days.

Socially I am not sure that the players on that championship team hung out together. We had different friends and interests. But I do remember going out with Eddie Martin and some of his buddies to a bar in Pelham after a game. We got loaded on beer. I was happy when he was named All County in Westchester as the best right-handed pitcher. He was the most consistent guy that was out there. There's no question about it.

What I do remember are some of the ball fields we played on. Gedney Field on Mamaroneck Avenue in White Plains was one. Pelham Field, right next to the Hutchinson River Parkway, was another. I recall getting hit in the head with a thrown ball while I was running to first base at Memorial Field.

I wasn't the fastest guy but was a pretty good defensive third baseman. I did steal a base against White Plains once. I led the team in doubles that year because basically most of my power was to right center. Probably, if I was a little faster, some of those doubles could have been triples.

I have to tell you, over the years, my grandchildren, after hearing these stories, think that I was good enough to play in the major leagues.

I was born in the Bronx and moved to Mount Vernon in the fourth grade. My parents, a sister four years younger than me, and brother 12 years younger, lived at 82 Sheridan Avenue in a house right around the corner from Traphagen Elementary School.

My dad, Sydney, was in the retail appliance business in the Bronx. His business became successful and that led him and my mother, Elaine, to move to the suburbs of Mount Vernon, a growing community with grass and trees. It was delightful.

In our neighborhood, Little League wasn't the big thing. In my early years I remember having catches with my father all the time in the backyard. My dad was a world class speed walker who even won an event at the Millrose Track Meet at Madison Square Garden. He had an opportunity to represent the United States in the Olympics but because of financial issues he did not pursue it. Even though he was a competitor, I think I took to athletics because I felt comfortable with sports.

Sometimes when I return to that neighborhood, I'm shocked when I see how small everything is compared to where I raised my own children. Everything seems so small. Even to this day, I still get off the Cross County Parkway and drive by just to see the neighborhood and how it has changed. Some things come back to me. At other times, it seems as if I never lived there.

Mike Abrams, left, with Eddie Martin.

In the fourth grade, the dirt field at Traphagen playground was where we went. It was the place where you made your reputation. Sports were important. That's how they knew who you and what you were.

We pedaled to the school yard on our bicycles with our four-finger baseball gloves curled around the handlebars. Some of the kids who were a little more affluent had English racers; the others had Schwinns.

We didn't have to call anyone to play. Everybody knew where you would be on a Saturday morning. They would just show up.

The games started in the fourth grade with the same bunch of guys. You always knew who was going to choose who. There was always a game going on.

Kids would come down with their bats. We'd play all day and then go home. Occasionally, we would take one of the buses, the F bus or the G bus, into Mount Vernon where we would eat at The Broken Drum off Gramatan Avenue.

When I moved to Mount Vernon, we played stickball. It wasn't like the stickball played in the Bronx where you would hit for sewers. In Mount Vernon there was a tunnel beneath the Cross County Parkway near my house on Sheridan Avenue where we played stickball. Later, we moved the game to the parking lot at Traphagen Elementary School.

The key to those games was that we didn't use a Spaldeen. We used a tennis ball. If the fuzz was off the tennis ball, it was like throwing a hardball. The shaved ball, with the nap off of it, broke more sharply than others; no one knew why. It was much more difficult to make a hardball break than it was a tennis ball. I remember what I could do with that ball throwing screwballs and knuckleballs.

In those days, I wasn't involved in the Little League because I went away to sleep-away camp during the summer like many of my friends. But I do recall when there was a Little League team practicing at one of the fields. They came down with their uniforms. Our team looked like the Bad News Bears. They thought they were going to whip us. I don't recall the exact score, but we destroyed them.

Growing up I used to play all the time with Jimmy Gross, a high school teammate. I speak to him occasionally now, and we reminisce about how simple things were then. There was a certain security in those days. I remember running through my background to the Traphagen school yard. We used to spend eight and nine hours there playing ball. It wasn't organized. We just played and loved it.

It's totally different now. The kids today are programmed. They go from one activity to the next. They have coaches. That's why they are bored. My oldest grandson was a starting basketball forward for Horace Greeley High School in Chappaqua. Everything was organized. He played 12 months a year with coaches. Kids don't congregate in the playground anymore. They are missing a certain bonding.

For us, playing ball in the fourth grade was informal. We would just get together. Then we began entering a team in the Mount Vernon recreation league. It was basically neighborhood versus neighborhood.

Softball games eventually turned into hardball games. There once was a ball field not too far away from my home called Baker Field. It was located on California Road. Now Mount Vernon High School occupies that field. We entered a team called the Scorpions and we would play teams from Pelham and other locales.

One character who is instilled in my memory even to this day was an umpire. His name was Jake. Jake was something else. He loved kids. Jake was part of what we did. He was a great guy. He would arrive at Baker Field with two or three bats and catchers equipment. That was what we played with. Jake would stand behind the mound and be the only umpire for the day.

We all had our positions to play. Initially, I was a pitcher but moved over to third base and then to shortstop. Jimmy Gross pitched and also and at times would catch. Mike Richman, Skippy Baum, Steve Danetz, Kenny Lazar were also teammates. These were kids who lived in our neighborhood. We had gone through elementary school and then junior high school together.

I remember vividly playing in those rec games. I pitched a number of no-hitters and spent a great deal of time writing the score and date on the baseballs. I gave most of them to my grandchildren.

After the recreation league, we moved up to the high school on Gramatan Avenue and expanded our friendships. We met kids from other elementary and junior high schools from all corners of Mount Vernon. We started playing ball with them.

But we always returned to Traphagen to play ball. You always knew your friends would be there. In those days, the game we played was two-man or three-man softball. That's where there were two or three guys on a team. We would pitch to our own teammates. If you had a shortstop, he would cover the entire left side of the infield. If a ball went through, it was a single or double. You didn't run the bases. The key was whoever could hit the black top was a slugger. That was the thing to do.

Richie Shapiro: "Until the day he died in 1998 at the age of 57 he was the closest and best of friends."

We all played with spikes, Kangaroo spikes. There was a sporting goods store in Mount Vernon called Tom Godfrey on Gramatan Avenue that later moved to Fourth Avenue. I remember going there with my father, who bought me my first glove, a Rawlings PM baseball mitt. I was ecstatic about that glove because a Rawlings PM was the in-thing to play with. All baseball gloves then were substantially smaller than they are today. My glove, it seems, was almost always attached to me. I think I slept with it. I put a ball in it, oiled it, and did everything with it. I still have that leather-worn glove.

It is the kind of thing that I sit with and show my grandkids. They don't pay too much attention to the glove. I did take several grandsons to the Baseball Hall of Fame in Cooperstown, and they were amazed about the old equipment.

What I remember about our equipment is that when we played in the school yards, we didn't have baseball uniforms. We played in our khaki pants. We just played in white t-shirts with the jeans rolled up. So when I made the high school team, I was excited that I finally had a baseball uniform. The emblem on our uniform had the same large letter D that appears on the Detroit Tiger's shirt. I remember how heavy the uniform was.

Growing up in Mount Vernon was something else. Remember, it was the 1950s. So life was simple. I loved it because everyone was part of a community. There was an intangible thing. There was a certain bonding going on. Maybe we were all very idealistic, or maybe we did not know any differently. In looking back it was a very secure time of my life.

A lot people felt the same way as I did. There was something very special about growing up there. Mount Vernon wasn't a big community. It wasn't a small community either. It was the timing of everything. I think certain things we experienced as children are things that kids today just can't identify with. Exactly what it is I can't tell you. Life was simpler then.

We were brought up without a sense of entitlement. Most of our families had progressed, and our parents were living a life that their parents never lived. It was totally different. That's what Mount Vernon created for us.

After graduating from high school I played for a team called Knickerbocker Beer near Yankee Stadium. At one point I tried out for a team in the Sound Shore League and that didn't work out. Basically, I realized what my limitations were after playing in high school.

I went to Boston University and majored in accounting. I did play intramural and fraternity baseball, and when I graduated and ended up in the insurance business I played in several leagues in New York City's Central Park.

Till this day, I love getting into a batting cage. I can still hit. That's not a problem. Running is a little bit of an issue. I play with my grandchildren and still throw and catch. Until recently, I had all my old bats from high school, my Louisville Sluggers with my number on them. I think part of that is innocence and a way of looking back at the past. I think we all do a lot of that.

I'm married to my wife, Roberta, and we have one child. I also have three others from an earlier marriage.

I haven't missed a high school basketball game in years. My oldest grandson, Jesse Abrams, was the starting forward for Horace Greeley High School this year. What makes it nice is that many of the gyms we played in while at A.B. Davis High School 50 years ago, Jesse played in. So getting to his games never was a problem.

7 Neil Arena

My father, Augustino, was a cobbler, a shoemaker. He was some craftsman.

He actually did Lou Gehrig's shoes. Gehrig's wife, Eleanor, would bring his shoes down to my father's store in New Rochelle. Another Yankee, Frank Crosetti, did the same thing. Gehrig and Crosetti lived on the New Rochelle-Larchmont line in the Wykagyl area.

I was born in Mount Vernon Hospital and grew up at 131 South 12th Avenue. We lived in a duplex home; my grandparents lived on the lower floor and we lived upstairs. My mom, Gemma, was a housewife who stayed home and raised me along with my younger brother and sister.

Looking back, I think I really taught myself to play baseball since my dad wasn't the athletic type even though he played soccer. He spoke very little English.

When I was in Grimes Elementary School, I used to take a tennis ball or a Spaldeen when I was bored on a Saturday with nothing to do. I'd bounce the ball off our concrete stoop. The ball would come off each step differently. I would just keep throwing it and throwing it and try to follow the ball back to me. It taught me how to field when the ball came to my left, right, up, down or over my head. It was really cool.

But basketball, even as a youngster, was my favorite sport. I had a real penchant for the game, a real love for it. Baseball was really a bore for me. The only reason I played it was because everyone else around the corner played it: Jimmy Pucillo, Joe and Jimmy Kupfersteiner, and Davey Edwards. We were all on the Indians in the Little League and five of my friends on that club made the all-star team.

Neil Arena: "Basketball, even as a youngster, was my favorite sport."

Grimes was right around the corner from our house. I used to bounce my basketball to school and then play hoops with guys like the two Lewis brothers. One was Joe, who may have been about 6-feet 5-inches tall, and the other brother was a short stocky guy.

I remember we put a peach basket up on top of a pole across the street and then shot at the basket. I'll tell you, I had some eye. That's why I hardly ever used the backboard when I played high school ball for A.B. Davis. In my backyard, I used to shoot over the top of a clothesline because the yard was small. I figured I'd get it into the basket if I could arc the ball over the top of the clothesline the right way. That's how I got such an arc on my set shots when I was in high school.

I used to play with Ralph Castaldo. We knew each other since we were five years old. I was born on Seventh Avenue and then we moved to Ninth Avenue. I lived on the top floor and Ralph lived on the second floor of a house that his in-laws owned.

When I tried out for the Little League, that's where I met Eddie Martin. At the time, all my friends were already on teams. I could care less. My father got very upset about that because he knew I was a good ballplayer.

He said, "They're having a tryout because some of the teams need more players. I want you to go down there." "I don't want to go," I said. "Yes, you're going."

He took me down to Baker Field where there was a gang of kids. I reluctantly started pitching on the sidelines. A coach came over, saw some style and asked me, "What position do I like to play." I answered, "Short and second."

So he put me at second base. I remember someone hit a pop fly that was going to drop. I ran and dove for it and got it off the ground. That was it. The coach said to me, "I'm signing you up."

I was 11 at the time, and there were only three or four games left in the season. I thought that was a waste. But later I decided it was fun, and all my friends were on that team. So I only played one full year in Little League and made the All-Star team.

Early on I remember playing stickball with my friends around the corner. We'd play against teams from the Bronx since the Bronx line was only about half a block from our house on 12th Avenue. We used to go to the Mount St. Michael area and play guys there with the Spaldeen.

Anybody who hit it into Mr. Tucci's driveway had a grand slam. You see, we couldn't get the ball back. But there was a store nearby, so we could buy a Spaldeen for a quarter.

Looking back on our '59 championship baseball season, I remember that I had broken up with my girlfriend Maryann. I was very depressed.

Coach Bill Sywetz asked me, "What are you doing?" I said, "I don't want play baseball. I'm not into it." He said, "Come on. Come on out anyway. It will keep you busy."

I thought about it and realized that maybe he was right; maybe it would keep my mind off of this heartbreak. So I played.

We had a helluva defensive team. I played a lot of shortstop for Eddie Martin. The ball kept coming to me. I remember a play where our second baseman, Bruce Fabricant, threw it to me; it was a good toss. I just happened to bobble it, and then, all of a sudden, I gathered it in and tagged the base with the ball. I don't know why that play stuck in my mind, but it has.

I also remember Nicky Giordano's catch over the logs in left field that was incredible. There was also Martin's no-hitter. As much as I knew about baseball, I wasn't paying attention. I didn't even know he was pitching a no-hitter while it was going on.

I remember when I snapped my ankle in practice and was not able to play. I was learning how to slide and hook the bag to my left. I could always hook the bag to my right, but I could never drag my left foot across the bag to the outside of it toward right field.

Sywetz insisted that with my talent I should be able to do it. So I tried it and I snapped my ankle. I couldn't play second base for several games. I remember I had to hobble off the field. If I picked up a grounder, I couldn't put any weight on that left foot to throw. When I stepped down, I didn't have any power in the throw.

Arena played second base and shortstop for the Indians in the
Mount Vernon Little League.

But as I said, basketball was my favorite sport. I used to hide
the ball in a barrel at Grimes School. Then at lunchtime I'd go
down and get it and start shooting rather than go home to eat. I
used to go there on a Friday night, and the gas station guy, Larry,
would watch me shoot from across the street.

I was walking home one day with the ball and he asked me,
"Do you want me to put the light on there for you Neil? I can do
that. I can raise the light up and shine it on the basket." "You've
got to be kidding me," I said. "That would be great."

I came back after dinner and would shoot for an hour from the
same spot that I would shoot from the next day, and I'd drill it.

I played varsity for all the years I was at Washington Junior High School. I was in the seventh grade and tried out against the eighth-grade team like my grandson is doing right now. I remember making almost every shot during the tryout. The coach kept nodding his head at me.

It was the same thing in high school. I remember our center, John VonBargen, telling the coach, "Watch this kid shoot." Cliff Tetro was the JV coach. I didn't want to play three years of varsity because other older guys were there and I didn't feel it was fair. I would have been a seventh grader playing ninth grade ball. I didn't want to do that. I thought it was more fun just hanging out with my guys on the team.

In junior high we used to play against Jimmy Gross and that big guy, Mark Klein, and Jerry Fuchs, and Jimmy Schneider. They knew me and asked me, "Where was I going to go to high school?" I told them that I didn't know. They said, "Go to Davis. Go to Davis. We're going to Davis." I said that it was too far away, but I finally decided that if they wanted me to go there then I'd go.

Johnny Branca was the coach at Edison Tech in Mount Vernon. He wanted me to go to Edison since I lived on the south side. I wasn't mechanically inclined and couldn't see what I would learn at Edison. Then Irv Halstead saw me play Pony League ball. He came over to me and put his arm around me and said, "I'll see you soon at A.B. Davis Neil." I asked him why he said that. He replied," I want you to play basketball for me; I'm the coach."

So I went to Davis High School and don't you know it, Halstead leaves and Sully Mott becomes the new coach.

I was a guard. I relied on my quickness and my ball stealing and dribbling ability. I remember dribbling around when we didn't have the shot clock and having three or four guys chase me. I started at the top of the key, way out, and one guy was on top me. We were leading by one point. I started dribbling and he started chasing me. I got by him and went down to the middle of the key. Two guys started chasing me, and one finally grabbed me by my shirt in frustration.

I went to the foul line and made both shots. It was in the paper the next day. In my junior year I won the Con Edison award.

My best game was an away game at White Plains when I scored 33 points. I went 9 for 10 from the field and 15 for 17 from the foul line. In those days, that was a lot of points.

I also remember playing Roosevelt High School in a tournament at White Plains High School, and I almost beat them by myself. Their team only scored maybe 10 points more than I did. My teammates carried me off the court. My parents were at the game. It was the only game they ever saw me play.

On that team we had Jimmy Gross, Jerry Fuchs, Chico Coleman, Jimmy Schneider, and Jordan Hollingsworth, who transferred to Davis from Evander Childs in the Bronx. There weren't enough basketballs for him and me.

I remember playing with two pairs of socks. I'd wear the white socks underneath to absorb the sweat and the red ones on top of them. I know it was a joke that I kept a comb in my sock. It wasn't true. I would sweat so profusely that when I needed a haircut I'd wipe the sweat off the side of my hair and then wipe my socks. Our teammate, Mike Abrams, started that rumor.

Ironically, years later he came to a Rockland County basketball game I was refereeing and saw me brushing my hair or combing my hair during a time out. He walked over to me and said, "Nothing changes, right Arena?"

As a sophomore at Davis, I also sang with the Mello-Kings. If you were around during that time, then you'll remember that during the summer of '57 came a song, "Tonite, Tonite." The hit never climbed higher than number 77 in the US charts, but the single is still considered one of the greatest doo-wop tunes of all time.

The Mello-Kings consisted of brothers Jerry and Bob Scholl, Eddie Quinn, Larry Esposito, and me. We were all from Mount Vernon, and the group was formed in 1956. Eddie was the only member of the group I knew since he lived around the corner from me on Eighth Avenue. In the beginning, Jerry Scholl rehearsed several times a week at the Mount Vernon Boys Club.

Neil Arena, (fifth from l): "Tonite-Tonite was a great record but I never got a dime for it."

Later, a tryout was scheduled to find additional members. Larry Esposito joined the group. They were also looking for a baritone voice. So Frank Piccinini, who went to school with me, told me about the tryout. He was going to audition, too. I decided okay, I'll go to Larry's house on Columbus Avenue and audition.

I remember Larry played the piano by ear. I was an immediate fit for that group. The same thing happened when I tried out for a singing group in Virginia where I now live. Again it was a perfect fit.

I was on Dick Clark's television show American Bandstand twice. Clark also grew up in Mount Vernon and went to Davis. "Tonite-Tonite" was a great record but I never got a dime for it. When we met with the record company, we were told that we owed the company money for record sessions and other things. We were disappointed.

I loved growing up in Mount Vernon. It was competitive. There were a lot of great athletes there, and everybody knew each other. All those guys I played Little League and Pony League baseball with are still my friends, like Ralph Merigliano, Joey Adinaro, Johnny DeLisa, and Mike DeAngelo.

After high school, I went to Westchester Community College and played basketball there. I've been in the insurance business all my life. I'm still doing that in Ashburn, Virginia for Allstate Insurance. After my wife died, I moved to Virginia but get back to Westchester quite a bit to visit my son, daughter, and two grandsons. I think the grandkids have my genes. They are both good athletes.

8 *Bruce Fabricant*

Not too many people know it, but for about three years as a youngster all my friends called me Nellie. And to tell you the truth, I liked hearing that name a lot more than Bruce.

Ricky Libenson gave me the nickname. It was the summer of '52 when Ricky, Steve Matthews, and I were playing softball at Camp Ramaquois, in Pomona, New York. That's also when Jacob Nelson Fox, better known as Nellie, was coming into his own as the premiere second baseman of the decade. Now he is but a footnote in baseball history for younger fans. But let me tell you, Nellie Fox could play baseball. Few second basemen could hold his glove. He was one of the best contact hitters in baseball history. He seldom struck out and became an expert bunter. He made the American League All Star team 11 consecutive years, nearly all in the '50s. Who is to say that every era is a baseball golden age? The '50s was the top for baseball interest in New York as far as I'm concerned. And Nellie Fox was the best even though he played for the Chicago White Sox.

Baseball, as experienced by youngsters like me, was a game of heroes. Nellie Fox was my hero then and still is 56 years later. He was known for a huge wad of chewing tobacco in his left cheek and a ceaseless stream of infield chatter, nonstop hustle, and relentless determination to win. I wanted to be like Nellie Fox. I wanted to become that aggressive, take-charge leader in the infield. Ricky saw that and started calling me Nellie. The name caught on and everyone started calling me Nellie. He was my role model. He was a hero for small youngsters like me who had dreams of playing ball. I couldn't play ball enough.

I copied his style of play. Catch the ball with two hands and "feel the ball, feel the ball," he emphasized. I don't think anyone ever liked to play more than he did. In 1997, along with a friend Ed Hepner, I drove to Cooperstown to help celebrate Fox's induction into the Baseball Hall of Fame. I heard his widow say during the ceremonies "He played the game with all his heart, all his passion, and with every ounce of his being." I'd like to think that's how my high school teammates remember me.

Bruce Fabricant in backyard at 227 Claremont Avenue in 1945.

You can say I'm obsessive when it comes to Nellie Fox. I admit it. But it sure has given me a lifetime of joy. The walls in my White Plains office were adorned with Nellie Fox memorabilia; all of his baseball cards laminated and framed; autographed and framed pictures; and a 20 x 30-inch lithograph of baseball's "mighty mite".

Defense was Nellie's game. I wanted it to be mine also. A good glove enabled me to start seven games at second base during our championship '59 season. In that junior year, by my admission and everyone else's opinion, I was a good-field, no-hit player. To succeed and get playing time, I had to concentrate on making the routine plays over and over. What helped me were good hands, quick hands, to field balls that took erratic bounces or short hops.

Making the play was what mattered most to me. All of us on that team soon realized that defense wins championships. One of my most wonderful memories from the season was how a group of teenagers coordinated their efforts toward a common goal, subordinating themselves to achieve real teamwork. I tried to do that. We all did and I know it worked.

Steve Matthews, rear center, Bruce Fabricant, in uniform, Larry Briglia with bat, in Lincoln Elementary School.

We played the game the way our fathers and older brothers taught us on North 10th Avenue, South 12th Avenue, North High Street, Sheridan Avenue, and Union Avenue, as well as on playgrounds at Brush Park, Pennington Elementary School, Nichols and Traphagen Junior High Schools.

All of us on that team identified baseball with our childhood. My father, Morris, opened my heart to the game soon after we moved from the Bronx to a modest house at 227 Claremont Avenue. The house occupied a small plot of land that was separated from the Tramontano and Utall homes by narrow driveways and some grass. That was my world on Claremont Avenue, a tree-lined street and close knit homes that lay between Lincoln and Primrose Avenues. It was our playground, our park, our ball field. On weekends, I would dash outside to find my best friend, my neighbor, Bobby Tramontano. We would seek out our gang, Diane Camerino, Judy Cefalo, Martha Casner, and Janice Zimbardi. Riding our bikes, playing potsy, collecting piles of sand from the curb, and later playing a street game called hit-the-bat, filled our day.

As youngsters growing up we didn't realize that Mount Vernon was a divided city on the brink of northern style segregation. Many blacks from the South came to the north and settled in the city for better job opportunities and educational advancements. At the same time, many whites from the Bronx and Manhattan looked for a home in the suburbs in Mount Vernon. As a result, Mount Vernon became ethnically divided into two parts, north and south, by the New Haven railroad tracks of the Metro North railroad.

Since 1972, The A.B. Davis High School we knew has housed a middle school. Edison Tech closed in 1963 when its vocational department was combined with the new Mount Vernon High School on California Road. That was a result of federal lawsuit threatening a desegregation civil rights law suit. Bond issues failed in the late 1950's to build a new high school before they won approval to build the school.

Little of that mattered to our Claremont Avenue gang when

we were five years old. As Bobby Tramontano and I grew, we had catches across the lawns of both our houses or down the long strip of grass that separated our homes. When we got stronger we would throw a ball over our roofs to our backyards.

Bruce Fabricant

But it was from my father that I learned the game, how to play it, and how to appreciate it by reading as many books as I could about baseball's heroes and history. My father, Morris, was a short man. He had a dark complexion and didn't smile an awful lot. He called me "skeeziks", a pet name he had chosen. He was born in 1905, the year New York Giants' Hall of Famer Christy Mathewson won three games in the World Series. He died in 1986 the year of the Miracle Mets. For most of his 81 years he followed baseball. He taught me the game. He taught me to love it.

Fathers and sons, baseball and summer afternoons on the south side, north side, east side and west side of Mount Vernon was what the game was about. It was on our tiny front lawn, maybe 30 by 50 feet on Claremont Avenue, where my father tossed me my first ball. He taught me to keep my eye on it, to keep my glove low to the ground, and to watch the ball right into my glove. I felt I achieved something when I heard him say, "Good play." That said a lot.

He took me to my first Major League game in 1948 when we saw the Philadelphia Athletics play the New York Yankees at the Stadium. I don't remember who won. But as we walked through the tunnel ramp into the Stadium I saw one of the most beautiful sites in the world. There it was, Yankee Stadium, with its brown infield, green grass, and that façade ringing its rafters. Even today, I feel that same excitement when I walk into the Stadium for a night game. As we left the park that day in '48, I remember walking along the track that ringed the field as we exited through the center field bleacher area. I remember Manny's, a souvenir store on Jerome Avenue, and the toy I took home. But going to the game with my father was what I remember the most.

The 1955 Comets/Community Oil Little League team. Fabricant is third player from left in back row.

With my interest in baseball growing I would go to countless other games with him. Attending Yankee Stadium Old Timer Games were highlights. I'd squirm in my seat. I tried to name the old timer Mel Allen was introducing before he revealed his name. Old Timers Day at the stadium was revived at the Stadium in 1947 and has continued ever since, according to my friend Marty Appel, a former New York Yankee PR director. When co-owner Larry MacPhail revived it in '47, he called it second annual, citing Lou Gehrig Day as number one in 1939. I remember seeing Cy Young, who won more games (511) than most people see in a lifetime. He was honored in 1955 at Old Timers Day, one of his last appearances, when PR Director Bob Fishel escorted the 88-year-old Young onto the field.

I was an only child and my father left my child rearing mostly to my mother, Vera. The bond with my father was sports. I think it was like that with most of us growing up in that era. The two of us would talk about boxing and bicycling and baseball. Years later, every Friday night we would sit in front of the television and watch the Gillette Friday Night Fights. He would tell me stories about Jack Dempsey and Benny Leonard and Henry Armstrong. He would tell me stories about how he used to work for Bamberger's Department Store in Newark where he grew up and how he carried a sign around a boxing ring in Newark to signify each round. He would tell me about how he was a competitive bicycle racer at Newark's South Orange Avenue Velodrome. That was the Mecca of bicycle racing in America. He would talk about Bobby and Jimmy Walthour, Alf Goullet, all great riders of the '20s. He was so proud when he told me about the time he once beat Walthour as an amateur racer.

Until he died I had little proof that he was a bicycle racer. But that proof became evident when I went through his belongings and found a small photo of my father riding a bicycle on a 52 degree banked turn at the Velodrome. It might have been taken in 1921, 1922, or 1923. I had the photo restored and colorized. My daughter, Vicki, now has an enlarged print hanging on her basement wall while my smaller copy rests on a bookcase in my home.

By the late '40s we were one of the first families to have a television in our Claremont Avenue home. Sundays were baseball days in our home since my dad worked six days a week. In the '40s when all dry cleaning was done in cleaning plants rather than stores, my dad was partner of a Mount Vernon dry cleaning plant, Quality Cleaners. Next to the plant was a six bedroom, three-storied house at South Ninth Avenue. Mount Vernon's own Ralph Branca lived there. Years later another major leaguer, Ken Singleton, supposedly lived in the same house.

Bruce Fabricant: "All of us on that team identified baseball with our childhood."

On Sundays my dad and I watched doubleheaders on television. Between innings we would race outside. He would cross the street and stand in front a sloping plot of land and I would stand by a curb in front of our house. We would have a quick catch, maybe toss the ball back and forth 20 times, and then run back to the house to hear Mel Allen's description of the Yankee game.

By the time I was nine my dad thought I was ready for the Little League. I don't remember the tryout but I know I wasn't picked to play. A year later I was back at Hutchinson Field again on a freezing cold morning, the same Hutchinson Field we would call home in high school. I have very few memories about the tryout that I thought would seal my baseball fate forever. There out on the mound pitching to me on a bright sunny day was a huge man. It was Andy Karl and he was wearing a beautiful Boston Red Sox white home jersey with "Red Sox" emblazoned on the blouse. I would soon read about Karl, who was born in Mount Vernon, and played in the big leagues for Boston, Philadelphia Phillies, and Boston Braves from 1943-47. His 67 pitching appearances and 15 saves for the '45 Phillies were National League highs.

I must have hit Karl pretty good because the next thing I found out was that I made a team. I was a Comet. Our telephone rang several days later and Mr. Wisner was on the other end. He was my first coach and was telling my mother that he and his assistant, Mr. Kasner, would be over that night to drop off my uniform. When the doorbell rang there was Mr. Wisner holding my uniform. At that time it was probably the prettiest thing I had ever seen. It was folded as neat as a shirt display at Bloomingdale's Department Store. I was the happiest kid on our block.

Little League was fun. We were pretty good, Bobby Delmonico, Vonnie Wilkins, Mike Simon, and me. I lost contact with all my teammates after our two-year Little League career except for Bobby. I liked him a lot. In high school, he attended Edison Tech and we played against each other. To this day I regret not talking to Bobby whenever we played against each other. He played shortstop and I played second base. When an inning ended we would race off the field never looking or saying a word to each other.

In the early '50s we all had the luck to fall in love with baseball at the beginning of a great era. Since then baseball has played a role in my life and career. You see, baseball made me read. I always wanted to be a sportswriter. In 1951, my mother gave me a book, *Big Time Baseball*, which had stories about all the colorful personalities, records, famous players, blunders and big moments from 1900 to 1950 that endeared baseball to millions. I practically memorized the book and still have it in my baseball library.

What made that book unique was that it introduced me to reading. I found a subject I was passionate about. Finding something you're passionate about at an early age and reading about it can be a joy for the rest of your life.

When I picture my mother, I can see her sitting in our living room, reading, smoking, and sometimes holding a Vodka Collins in her hand. My mother was the one who turned me on to the world of books. My dad's interest in reading was limited to newspapers. A spring or summer highlight for me was taking a train ride with my mother into New York City. We would see a movie and then go to a bookstore to find something about baseball.

The few times I would get angry on those trips were when I had to get home for a late afternoon softball game at Traphagen Junior High School. I didn't want to be late. I would race to the playground on my bike. Back then I rode it everywhere, into town, to school, to the library, and to Baker Field. At Traphagen, that's where I learned to field grounders. That's where our friend Richie Shapiro gracefully tracked down fly balls. We all marveled how he went after them. That's where we played ball and were expected to learn the game the hard way, by ourselves, without specialized coaching.

At Traphagen, no one cared as much about baseball like Steve Matthews and I did. Our baseball loyalties were divided between the Yankees and Dodgers. He was a Dodgers fan. I've told him that if I had a chance to root all over again, I too would have been a Dodgers fan. Reynolds, Raschi, and Lopat. Erskine, Roe, and Labine. Campanella or Berra. Mantle or Snider. Sitting under a tree we would debate comparative lineups and pitching staffs. We were discussing our shared friendship when we talked about baseball.

After Traphagen, all of us moved on to A.B. Davis High School. I also moved to a new home at 44 Fleetwood Avenue near the high school. I'll bet there aren't too many people alive who know who A.B. Davis was. That grand old edifice on Gramatan Avenue that was named after him was built in 1912. At the turn of the century, the Mount Vernon high school was in the old Sophie J. Mee building on the city's south side. It then moved to the top floor of the old Lincoln Elementary School. The "hilltopper" school that we knew had additions in the '30s. By the '60s the building was gutted and the new Davis is the same only on the outside and perhaps in the auditorium. The football field behind the school has been truncated and the cement grandstands that hosted intercity games with Edison High School are long gone. And who was A.B. Davis? Abial Brown Davis, the principal of Mount Vernon High School for over 30 years, wouldn't recognize the area. The school was named after this Midwesterner in the late '30s after his retirement. Teammates might remember the somber portrait of the stern white-haired old man in the building named after him. He was an institution. Many of us still think the bronze statue in front of the building is A.B. Davis. Actually it is Teddy Roosevelt making a stump speech.

Bruce Springsteen had it right. Those were glory days at A.B. Davis High School for all of us. That's what those 49 days of spring baseball in '59 were all about. Today, only 16 of us are left who remember what we were like 50 years ago when we were champions. Over a lifetime I have partied and talked with my best friend Jay Howard countless times about our high school memories and sports accomplishments. He achieved quite a bit of individual success on Yonkers baseball diamonds and hardwood basketball courts while at Lincoln High School. We kid each other unmercifully. He put the numbers up and is proud of them. I can't say the same. But what I invariably point to is that I've accomplished the ultimate goal and that is winning a championship. That ended many conversations.

As I said earlier, I was a glove man, pure and simple. I loved turning a double play. I loved getting the ball quickly out of my glove and on to first base. When I played, my glove was an unusually small mitt. It was a Wilson Jim Finigan model A2111 buckle back glove. It wasn't a trendy PM model. Finigan's five year career peaked as a rookie in 1954 while playing for the Philadelphia Athletics. I found that glove in a toy store at the corner of Fisk Place and Park Avenue near the Mount Vernon train station. The glove probably was the smallest on the team. I didn't want the ball ever to stick or get lost in it.

The tattered and re-stitched glove remains one of my most prized possessions. It followed me to Michigan State in 1960 and intramural softball, and then back to the many Westchester County softball diamonds in later years. In the Greenburgh Over Forty League, sometimes play would stop when a base runner got to second base and saw my mitt. He had to hold it and slap the pocket. Actually, there was no pocket. It was a flat piece of leather.

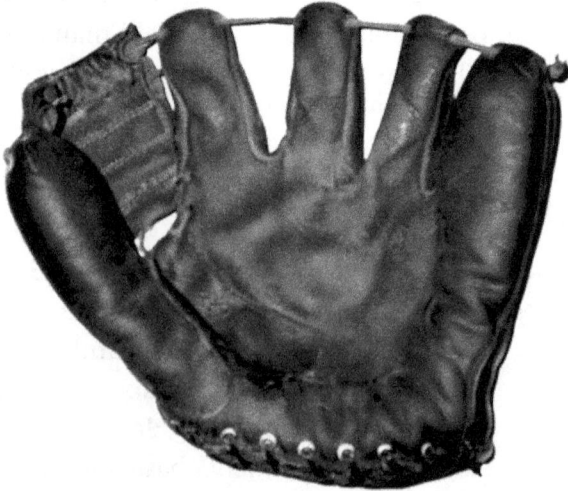

Bruce Fabricant: "The tattered and re-stitched glove remains one of my most prized possessions."

For me, playing second base in high school was all about quick feet, quick hands and some courage. I loved standing in there and getting a toss from Neil Arena, Eddie Martin, Mike Abrams, or Frank Fiore to make the double play and not worrying about being taken out. My arm wasn't particularly strong, so I compensated on double plays, by getting the ball out of my glove quickly. When I was 12, my dad and my Uncle Charlie hung a boxing speed bag from our basement ceiling. I'd practice with it daily and became pretty good at it. I'm sure it helped my hand-eye coordination. I later read Willie Randolph as a youngster did the same thing. I was fair game at second base. I made my throw, like my hero Nellie Fox, from the middle of the base bag. The only time I was nailed was in a game against Edison Tech when Donnie Neise took me out. I still remember the jeers and laughter from the Edison Tech bench.

But what I remember most about that season was infield practice. I couldn't wait for the wondrous chorus of infield chatter. Looking back, I've played a lot of golf, tennis, and softball. Nothing has given me more pleasure than taking infield practice. I couldn't get enough. Hitting could wait. Fielding fast-hopping grounders, throwing to first, running back to the second base bag to take the throw from the catcher, and then pivoting and throwing around the horn was heaven. So was turning double plays in practice from every conceivable angle. I also remember the anticipation before every pitch. All of us had different habits before each pitch. I would bend at the knees and thrust my glove to the ground. It was all about getting a good jump on the ball.

I think our good fielding plays in '59 were forgotten quicker than our pitching accomplishments. Years ago, baseball was all about defense and pitching. I liked that. But today, offense and the home run is what the game is all about. The free time I spent playing ball in the Traphagen school yard was invaluable in helping me learn to field. Even though I enjoyed Little League there really was no room for imagination. At the school yard I could pretend to be Nellie Fox in this situation and that situation. I could make play after play.

Even as a 10-year-old, I considered myself a heady player, whether it was taking the extra base, or throwing to the right base. When we played in the schoolyard, the biggest mistake Steve Matthews, Bobby Weiner, Richie Shapiro, or I could make was to forget. We could all make errors and flub a ground ball. We couldn't forgive mental errors, even back then. Being a smart baseball player meant as much to me as getting a B grade in Miss Reynold's seventh grade math class. I even think it carried as much weight with my friends. In high school I remember the misery of making a bonehead play. Whenever I drive by Gedney Field on Mamaroneck Avenue in White Plains, I stare at the field and remember a sunny afternoon game. I was picked off second base with the bases loaded. The trot back to the bench seemed forever.

Bruce Fabricant: "What I remember most about that season was infield practice, those ground balls, and wondrous chorus of infield chatter."

Memories have blurred about details of the 15 games we played in '59. There are two however, that occupy a corner of my mind. Early in the season we beat Commerce High School of Yonkers 1-0. Commerce was threatening with Rich Todd on third and Bruce Manning on second. Eddie Martin was pitching, and the two of us exchanged signals. Eddie turned and wheeled and threw a strike to me at second base. We nabbed the runner to kill the rally. The joy of baseball, winning baseball, burst out from within me as I ran off the field to end the inning.

Four games later I helped in another hard fought victory, scoring the winning run in a 2-1 win over Yonkers High School. I walked to open the top half of the fifth. Lenny Henderson hit sharply to the Yonkers' first baseman Lou Fariello. He failed to come up with the ball cleanly. I took off and came around all the way from first base to score. Speed may be in your genes, but I'd like to think all the times I raced home on my bike for lunch and then back again to the school yard to play ball helped strengthen my legs.

I wasn't the only one on the team who remembers that dash. Eddie Martin remembered it also. Forty years after the game Eddie gave me the book he wrote about his Hartsdale Pet Cemetery, *Dr. Johnson's Apple Orchard.* On the inside cover he inscribed, "To Bruce, thanks for hustling home in the Yonkers game, Eddie".

Baseball author Lawrence Ritter once said, "The best part of baseball is the past." I couldn't agree more. Everyone on our team has played the inner game, baseball in the mind. I know I have. It's all about remembering, going back to the past, and picturing what once was. On a warm Saturday morning in the early spring of 1999, on the 40th anniversary of our championship season, I went back to visit the baseball diamond of our high school youth, Hutchinson Field. I sat in the bottom row of the same metal stands along the first base line just as we did four decades earlier.

Some baseball diamonds never change. The Hutchinson skin infield with its hard, baked dirt hadn't changed much. Splotchy green grass still covered the outfield. The oil tanks near the creek in right center field were still there. They seemed smaller. The incinerator smokestacks down the right field line were gone. That didn't matter. I was home again.

Watching youngsters throwing a ball brought back memories of that '59 spring when a group of guys from all corners of Mount Vernon played together for one glorious high school baseball season. When it was over we were champions of the Westchester Interscholastic Athletic Association. We beat the biggest schools in the county, New Rochelle, White Plains, and Yonkers.

Bruce Fabricant: "He was like the little engine that couldn't, but he did."

Individuals and events flash back, even now fifty years later. I can still see my teammates. For baseball purists everywhere, Willie Mays' catch off Vic Wertz' drive in the 1954 World Series was a play for all time. But I'll never admit it was any better than Nicky Giordano's grab in left field that saved Eddie Martin's no hitter. I can still see Teddy Cardasis at bat, tall and elegant like Ted Williams, and Tommy Ambrosino banging out hits at a team leading .379 clip. Then there was Eddie Martin, Westchester's best right hander, who compiled a 7-0 record. Thirty-six years early, in 1943, another A.B. Davis right hander, Ralph Branca, won seven straight games to lead his team to the same WIAA championship.

Were we a great team? I don't think so. In fact, we might not have been the best team in the county in '59. But we were champions. We were in most games. We found the cutoff man. We hit to the right side to move runners along. We bunted all the time. We got the job done with a wonderful combination of speed and daring on the base paths, a solid defense and superb pitching. And the best part of it all that year was that we liked each other. Nothing inspires camaraderie like sharing a win, not only of a game, but of a season.

Ten years ago I was curious how our strong pitching and good defense combined to create a winning season, a 12-3-1 season. I went back to the Mount Vernon Public Library and looked through the Mount Vernon Daily Argus microfilm that divulged statistics from each game. Looking back through those box scores was like opening a family album. Here was everybody from our high school baseball family.

I found out we were a team that simply would not be beaten; a team that seldom walloped anyone but habitually scored just enough runs to win. Power hitters batted elsewhere that season. Can you believe this, through a 16 game schedule, A.B. Davis High School did not hit one home run. The team only managed one triple.

I also found out that coming off a mediocre 8-5 season in 1958, first-year Coach Bill Sywetz had few returning seniors and quite a few unproven juniors. Our longest winning streak was six games, capturing the last 10 out of 11 games. In my three years of high school that '59 team was the school's only championship squad.

And wouldn't you know it, 1959 was Nellie Fox's greatest year. He led the White Sox to its first American League pennant in 40 years, and he was selected as the American League's Most Valuable Player. Having the third lowest batting average and the fewest home runs in the American League, the White Sox relied on speed, defense, and pitching. So did us that same year. We batted .240 for the season and averaged only 4.5 runs per game. Our opponents however batted only .180 against us and averaged but 2.8 runs and 4 hits per game.

Playing baseball after that season never had the same intensity for me. I graduated in 1960 and went on to Michigan State University and majored in journalism. After serving two years in the military I found my first job at Grey Advertising in New York City. On the first day of work I also found my best friend and partner for life, my wife, Bobbi.

In those early working years I was lucky and had a job that combined business with my passion for baseball. I often sat in the Yankee dugout interviewing Getty Oil Honorary Yankee Batboys and then moved on to the press room to write stories for newspapers throughout the New York metropolitan area. In 1970 I worked with the New York Mets' Tug McGraw and wrote and produced a film for Panasonic called *"Bullpen"* that traced growth of baseball's relief pitchers. I've seen the film on television, and there is a print in Baseball's Hall of Fame.

Raising two girls in Ardsley, Robin and Vicki, my wife, Bobbi, and I watched them compete in softball games, soccer and swimming. Now, Robin and her husband Joseph Pagano, along with our daughter Vicki, and her husband Scott Jeffery, watch their children and our grandchildren, Madeline, Sophie, and Kate somersaulting and jumping on gymnastic floors.

In 2007, I went to a New York Yankee game at the Stadium. It was 59 years after I held my father's hand and walked into that same Stadium. This time I was holding my grandson Cole's hand just as my father held mine nearly six decades earlier. We were walking from a parking lot to meet Cole's father, Scott. The three of us sat in the stands watching the Baltimore Orioles defeat the Yankees 7-6 that August night. Sitting there brought back memories of walking around the Stadium's field in 1948 with my dad. It was a magic night. There really was a bond between generations. Cole never met his great grandfather Morris, my dad. I'm sure that night there was something that tied our generations together.

Bruce Fabricant

While I never knew the score of the first game I saw Cole didn't have the same problem. I made sure of that. We created a big sign before we got to the Stadium, *"My First Yankee Game."* At the bottom of the first inning, the image of Cole standing on his seat next to us, holding up his sign appeared on television. Many of our friends and family saw it. Announcer Michael Kaye was telling his viewers that it was a shame the youngster was seeing his first game and watching the Yankees lose. I don't think so. That photo is now framed along with the box score. That's what baseball can do for you.

9 *John Fortier*

There aren't many youngsters who get a chance to pitch to a major league player. I did.

When I was playing for The Standards in the Mount Vernon Pony League, my coach told me that Ralph Branca wanted to come down and have me pitch to him.

"Hey, that's great. I'll do it," I told my coach. It sounded like a nice experience.

So the following week, Branca, who played for Davis in the early '40s and later, of course, for the Brooklyn Dodgers, came down, and we threw the ball around. I had a nice talk with him afterwards.

He told me, "Nice job. Keep at it. Keep trying and see how far you get." It was a nice experience. I've never forgotten it.

Growing up, I really never had an adult teach me how to play ball. I was blessed with a strong arm, so I guess that's how I developed into a ballplayer. My dad, John, and mom, Gwendolyn, moved to the Fleetwood section of Mount Vernon when I was about four or five. I was born in Yonkers. We moved to the apartments at 445 Gramatan Avenue, not far from the high school.

Dominick Sposato, Bill Seltman, and I started played stickball in the parking lot behind the apartment. A lot of the guys I played with didn't go to the Mount Vernon public schools. They went to Catholic schools. I went to Lincoln School and played in the playground there. Then, in the sixth grade, I went to Nichols and played ball with friends like Raymond Gore and Billy Bird.

John Fortier: "Ralph Branca, after catching me, said nice job, keep at it, keep trying and see how far you get."

I never played in the Mount Vernon Little League. First, there wasn't anybody where we lived who tried to get me interested in playing. Second, my mom had pretty strict reigns on me back then, so I couldn't travel far from home. Little League games weren't played in the Fleetwood area.

So it wasn't until I started playing in the Pony League that I faced real pitching in an organized game. I had a pretty good arm, so my coach made me a pitcher. And when I wasn't on the mound, I was in the outfield or caught. I had no idea how to pitch from a stretch. Once somebody got on base they usually were able to steal on me. I missed getting instruction. That was the main thing I remember growing up.

I'll tell you the truth. When I was coming up through high school in my sophomore year, Irv Halstead was the baseball coach. He brought me up at the end of the season for the last game, just to get a taste of it. I remember that. I was disappointed when he retired because I wanted to play for him. I didn't really enjoy playing for Coach Sywetz mainly because I didn't learn anything from him. I wasn't into our team that much either, even though we had a very good season. I would have liked to have gone further than just playing high school ball.

I was the only player on our championship team to play all three outfield positions that season. I'll tell you what happened. Teddy Cardasis came up to the varsity. He was a year behind me. He was our best athlete. I remember playing softball with him in the park on Broad Street in Fleetwood. We were both pretty good outfielders, so Coach Sywetz wanted to get both of us in the lineup at the same time. So that's why he switched us around.

I played in all 16 games that season. I was in center field for four of the first five games and really didn't hit well. When we beat White Plains later in the season, I drove Mike Abrams in with a single. I remember stealing home in that game.

The biggest claim to fame in my baseball career came when we played Suffern in an important game late in the season. The game went nine innings and Eddie Martin pitched them all. I just remember Eddie pitching terrifically all the time. Early in the game, I singled home Bruce Fabricant after he walked and stole second. Then in the top of the ninth, I walked and stole second and third base. There was a passed ball and I slid home with the tie-breaking run. We won that game 3-2.

In the next game we beat Concordia 10-4. I remember hitting a double with the bases loaded to drive in three runs. I guess you can say I finally hit my stride late in the season. In our last game against Edison Tech, I drove in another run. What's interesting about that game is that I was the catcher. Tony Cioppa had caught the first 15 games of the season, and for some reason the coach held him out in the last game. He put me in, but I really didn't like to catch.

Fortier played for the Standards in the Pony League in 1956.

After graduating I went to Iowa State University in Ames, Iowa. I was interested in forestry, and Iowa State was one of the schools that taught it. I tried out for the baseball team, but first I hurt my knee and then my shoulder. There was a good chance I was going to make the team although I probably wouldn't have played. That was the end of my baseball career.

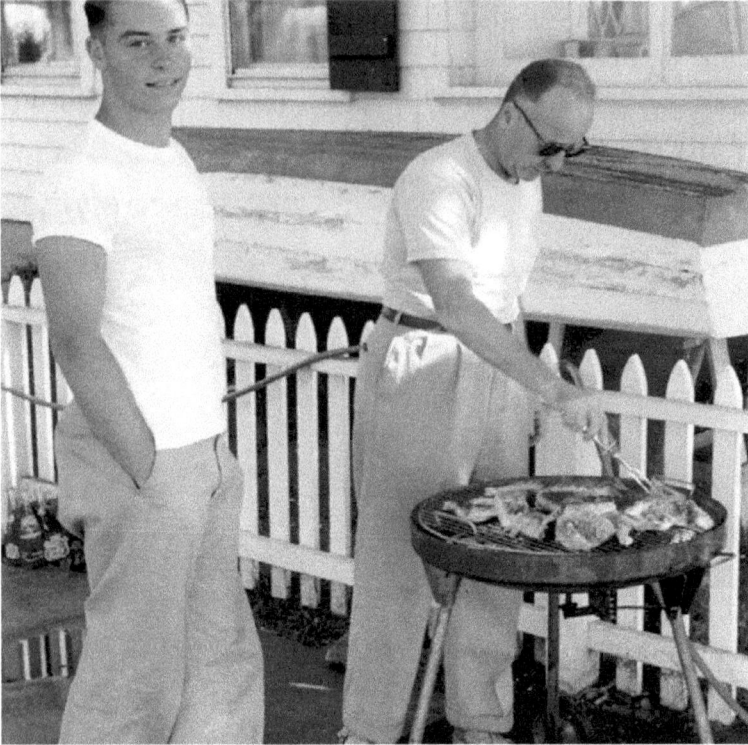

Fortier and his father, John, in 1958. He was the only player to play all three outfield positions on the championship club.

After I graduated from Iowa State, I worked in southern Illinois for a couple of years and then came back to Fleetwood and worked for a plant research organization, Boyce Thompson Institute. I got married and the job with Boyce ended when the Institute moved to Cornell in Ithaca, New York. I had an opportunity to work there, but my wife, Nancy, and I decided not to go. We did move up to the Glens Falls, Saratoga area. We've been there for the last 30 years. That's where we raised our three children, Sean, Kristen, and Kate.

10 *Ernie Motta*

I can make you mine, taste your lips of wine, any time, night or day.
Only trouble is, gee wiz, I'm dreamin' my life away
I need you so that I could die, I love you so, and that is why
Whenever I want you, all I have to do, is
Dream, dream dream dream, dream

Remember that song *All I Have to Do Is Dream* from the Everly Brothers? Boy was it popular song in 1958 and '59. One of my fondest memories about our championship season was singing that song on bus rides to away games.

I started singing it. Then Teddy Cardasis began harmonizing with me. Then everyone on the team joined in. You could say the song became a good-luck charm. It was like I said, "OK, we think we can win this thing." And we did.

While I've been living in Stamford for the past 20 years, I still run into people from Mount Vernon. I work out at the Tully Health Center there. A couple of years ago our teammate Eddie Martin gave each of us an A.B. Davis Championship tee-shirt. I'm wearing the tee-shirt at the gym and a fellow comes over to me, and asks, "Where did you get that shirt?" I said "We had a reunion of our '59 championship team." He said, "Really, you're an A.B. Davis graduate?" I said, "Yes." He said, "Class of '54." That happens quite a bit to me.

The best story is that my daughter lives in north Stamford.

She got a contract for a movie that they filmed in Stamford. For six days they shot part of the film in her house. I went to watch the filming there and the prop director is setting stuff up and my daughter says, "Daddy, Daddy. This guy came from Mount Vernon." That turned into an hour's conversation for me with the prop director about the old days. I found out that his sister went to A.B. Davis. We talked about Fourth Avenue, the Bee Hive Restaurant and all the great basketball players that came from Mount Vernon.

Ernie Motta: "I remember his big curve ball where batters would duck as the ball curved over the plate."

Mount Vernon may have a tarnished reputation today. But it still has such a rich environment. It was great growing up there.

I was born there. We lived at 454 South Seventh Avenue in a four-family house. Previously, my mother's father had a fruit store on the bottom floor. Then they converted it into a four-family house. I lived there with my parents, my aunts and uncles, my sister and five cousins. That's quite a bunch.

From kindergarten through sixth grade I went to Nathan Hale

and then moved on to Washington Junior High School. There I knew quite a few fellows from Little League and Pony League who later became my high school teammates.

The neighborhood on South Seventh Avenue was something. Everyday we would ask, "What are we playing today, baseball, football?" We had a backyard with a basketball hoop and net. The side alley next to the house is where I learned to play stickball. Remember that pink Spalding ball? I started to learn how to pitch there. That's where I began throwing curve balls.

My mother, Jean, was a seamstress. My father, Andrew, worked for Yale & Towne Lock Company in Stamford where he poured molds. Here's some about the company you may not know. Yale & Towne Manufacturing Company was established in 1868 by Linus Yale and Henry Towne. Linus Yale was the inventor of the tumbler lock. The company would become the leading manufacturer of locks in the world. Yale & Towne at one time was the leading employer in the Stamford, Connecticut, area.

My father was a baseball player. There is a new book out about the history of New Rochelle. There is a section in it about a semi-pro team called the New Rochelle Robins. For more than 50 years, the Robins have been the dominant team in semi-pro baseball in the New York metropolitan area. The team has routinely produced powerhouse ball clubs, featuring dozens of top college and former pro ballplayers.

Besides serving as a Robins' coach, my dad and his four brothers played on the team in the 1940s.

He loved baseball. He watched it constantly and played baseball with me whenever he could. I remember when I was six years old he put a bat in my hand and pitched to me for the first time.

Our entire family was geared to baseball. Every time we visited a cousin we played ball. We all loved the New York Yankees. My father wouldn't talk about any other team. As a youngster, Whitey Ford and Bullet Bob Turley were my favorites. I even tried copying Turley's windup. They don't use windups like that anymore. I don't know why.

I don't remember getting my first baseball glove. But, to tell you the truth, my father had so many old mitts. They were the ones that just covered the hand. He used to give me his hand-me-downs. I started out with one of those.

Summer time meant baseball on our street. We played bunting in the backyard using either a Spalding or a softball. Some one would try to hit it past you and run around the backyard. It was great because it helped us develop the ability to field a short bunt. We did that a lot. Then we graduated to stickball.

I always was a pitcher. That goes back to when I was ten years old. My father put down a rubber plate in the alley way next to our house. That's where he taught me how to pitch.

He was catcher. He encouraged me to try out for the Little League when I was eight years old. The Little League then was a lot different than it is today. I remember in my first year getting up to bat against a pitcher named Goody Bradford. He was twelve. He threw a monster fastball. I was shaking.

I had a cousin, Fred Corrado, who was on my team. He was older. In later life he became president of Planter's Peanuts. Anyway, when I was up at bat, he was screaming at Goody Bradford, "Don't hurt him. Don't hurt him." Meanwhile, I'm shaking. I swung the bat and hit the ball. I was so surprised. Everyone in the stands were yelling, "Run, run." I remember that so vividly.

We were called The Eagles. There weren't any high teammates on that club. One fellow we graduated with, Bill Bauersfeld, was on the team. His father coached the team, and my father helped him out coaching.

It was quite a league. Larry Townsend, who later pitched in our senior year at A.B. Davis, was in the same league.

I don't remember too much about our regular Little League seasons. I played four years of Little League ball, from 8 through 12 years of age. We played on quite a few diamonds like Longfellow School and then later at Brush Park and at Hutchinson Field.

*Ernie Mott (bottom row, third from r) pitched for the Eagles in
Little League. His dad, Andrew (top row l), coached the team and
played for the New Rochelle Robins.*

Between Little League games we played stickball right next
door to our house, which was right next door to a Baptist church.
I remember breaking more than one church window with a
batted ball. Sometimes my folks had to pay to fix those windows.

Even in Little League my curve ball was my out pitch. But I
remember one time years later when my curve didn't work.

It was the tenth game of our championship 1959 season, and
we played Yonkers' Roosevelt High School at Hutchinson Field.
In the second inning, Roosevelt's first baseman, Ron Rothstein,
who was an All County basketball player and later played for the
University of Rhode Island, led off. I struck him out. There were
quite a few fans sitting in the bleachers. There was a fellow
named Steve watching the game. He had a mouthful of braces
and was heavy set and had a crew cut. He must have been a
friend of Rothstein's. I can still see Steve laughing away when I
struck him out.

But the next time Rothstein came to bat, I threw him a curve.
He just waited for it. He hit a towering home run over Lenny
Henderson's head in right field. We lost that game 5-1. Our

centerfield, Teddy Cardasis, had two hits and drove in our only run.

Mount Vernon was a great city to grow up in. I remember every Saturday walking up and down Fourth Avenue past Genung's Department Store and Buddies clothing store.

People talk about poor people. I guess we were poor. We lived in the south side of Mount Vernon, which was fully integrated in the 1950s. There was a great deal of camaraderie. My best friend in those early years was Bobby Reid, an African American, who later went to Edison Tech. Another friend was Tommy Wynn who also was African American. He went to A.B. Davis, then college, and eventually got his PhD.

Bobby, Tommy and I played anything, every day, every season. It was basketball and then football and baseball in the backyard. We mostly played in the yard and on the street. It was like a big playground. You always had someone around to play with.

That is different than what kids face today. My wife, Judy, and I raised two girls, Andrea and Laurie Beth. My oldest grandson plays hockey. Sarah Palin made the hockey mom famous. It is so true. Sports today are so organized, maybe too organized. My daughter takes her son three times a week to practice or play in games. We used to be able to organize a game just like that. We could find nine kids to play at the spur of the moment. In the suburbs today it is different. Mom has to drive the youngster everywhere.

Don't get me wrong. It isn't all bad today. My little granddaughter Maya loves baseball. She has a great swing. She got into Little League baseball and was picked for an All Star team in Stamford. She was the first girl to ever be picked on the league's All Star team. That created quite a controversy. The league didn't know if they were going to allow her to play, but they finally did. So see, things do work out.

I was 3-3 on our '59 championship team. Even though we won it all that year, it was the worst pitching season I ever had. That goes for Little League, Pony League or high school ball.

Coming into that junior season I hadn't lost a game in any

league. I was 7-0 on our high school junior varsity team. During that summer recreation league I threw three one-hitters and a no-hitter.

We started the '59 season playing Nyack, and we had a terrible game there. I lost the opener 6-4 and then lost again to Rye 9-3. Rye was a good team. They were tough. There's no doubt I was a little down.

People talk about pitching, and each pitch is what you work for. I don't believe you have any preconceived notions about a team or a player. You just try and make the pitch. It's each pitch that counts. You get people out. That's the name of the game. So what happens when I lost, they hit me.

But we came back, and I pitched a complete game in beating White Plains 5-2 at home. If you look at the record, I always beat White Plains and New Rochelle. I don't think I ever lost to them. Against White Plains I gave up seven hits, struck out three and didn't walk anyone. Nicky Giordano, our left fielder, had a big game. He doubled in the fifth inning, driving in Eddie Martin and Tony Cioppa.

We then picked up our sixth win in eight games in beating Yonkers' Lincoln High School 7-5 at Memorial Field. Lincoln was a mediocre team. I went five innings allowing three runs on three hits to pick up the win. In the bottom of the third inning, we scored five runs on singles by Martin, Cioppa, Cardasis, Tom Ambrosino, and a double by Mike Abrams.

In our next to last game of the season we played Concordia Prep at Bronxville. We beat them 10-4 and I threw a five-hitter. I remember Abrams, who played third, had quite a game. He had two doubles and walk. So that's how I ended up 3-3.

My father came to nearly every game. Matter of fact, at a pre-season game against Pelham Memorial High School he was asked to umpire. He umpired from behind the pitchers mound, right behind me.

After the game our coach Bill Sywetz saw me going home with my father and said, "I didn't know it was your father." I said, "Yeh, he is my dad." He said, "Good job umpiring."

Outfielder Richard Giloth.

There also were times when I was supposed to bat during a game, and our coach wanted to pinch hit for me. Everybody on our bench yelled out, "No, let him hit, let Ernie hit." More times than not, he let me hit.

What I recall about that championship club is being surprised about Eddie Martin and how well he pitched. I don't remember him as a pitcher in the Little League or Pony League. Maybe he was. But I don't remember that. He started in '59 and had a sinker type pitch. Nobody could hit him all season long. That surprised me the most. There's no doubt he really took us to the championship.

The team was solid. We had good players. I remember early in the season Richie Shapiro, a great basketball player, pitched for us. He had a strong arm. But he didn't know where the plate was. I guess the coaches wanted him to get another school letter and tried making him into a pitcher. Baseball never was his game. He didn't have a background in it.

As far as our hitting went, the best hitter was Teddy Cardasis. He had everything. When Teddy was going into the Little League in Mount Vernon, there were eight teams. Then they expanded the league. Teddy and guys like Bruce Fabricant went into the expanded league.

Well, I used to read Teddy's Mount Vernon Daily Argus clippings. Teddy Cardasis batting .600. I couldn't believe reading about this guy. Then I met Teddy in high school for the first time. He could do it all. Another good hitter on our team was Tommy Ambrosino. He just hit singles and turned in the highest batting average on the team.

In school I hung around with Cardasis, Nick Giordano and Tony Cioppa. Tony is actually related to one of my wife Judy's cousins. He was a good catcher. He was a smart kid. Besides having an A average, he knew how to call a game. A catcher is very important. He was able to size up the players and what pitch to throw. I got very comfortable pitching to Tony.

Interestingly, after we won the championship, for many of us who were juniors at the time, our senior season was a downer. New people joined the team. Cioppa wasn't catching me any more. It wasn't the same. We didn't come close to winning anything. I had a 5-2 record our senior year.

There was a fellow who graduated before us, Larry Rauch. He was a good catcher. He played college ball and I think he played in the minor leagues. He came back one summer and said to me, "We wanted to hit against you because you had a professional curve ball." They practiced against me that summer.

Nowadays it is always the split finger. I never heard of that. I don't know what a split finger is.

After graduating from A.B. Davis I went to Iona. They wouldn't let freshmen play ball. I found Iona quite difficult my sophomore year since I was carrying 21 credits. I had to cut class in order to play ball. So I ended up losing interest in the game. I mostly sat on the bench. I did pitch one inning against Larry Bernarth, the former New York Mets pitcher, who was playing for New York University. That ended my career and I put the glove away finally.

It was time to work. After graduating from Iona with a degree in accounting, I landed my first job at ESSO Humble Oil in Pelham. I went back to Iona for a master's degree in accounting. Then I went to work for Aerosol Techniques in Connecticut, left that and got a job in Mount Vernon in the Pepsi plant on Sanford Boulevard. How coincidental was that. The plant was right next to the Hutchinson River ball field we played on. I was the comptroller of the plant and stayed there for about five years, finally moving on to Einstein Hospital in the Bronx as a deputy comptroller.

Teddy Cardasis: "I couldn't believe his Mount Vernon Daily Argus *Little League clippings."*

That started my career in the medical field working at Cornell Medical Center and then for 14 years at NYU Medical Center in Manhattan finishing up as director of finance. That's where I ended my working career. We've been living in Stamford for over 20 years.

11 *Bob Puccillo*

I played with a musical group called the Gay Notes. It was four of us. Donnie Heath is the only guy I remember. He sang with me and played drums. I played guitar. We had another guitar and piano player. We played for an assembly at A.B. Davis once when I was a junior and also played at quite a few dances in high school.

I remember Neil Arena and "Tonite-Tonite". I thought that was pretty neat. I wasn't in a band when I met him. I remember Neil playing basketball. We really didn't have much of an interface. But I remember that song.

I got into music but really wanted to play baseball. I didn't think I was too bad a pitcher. Looking back, it was my father who was the one who taught me how to play.

I was born in Morrisania Hospital in the Bronx, and we stayed in the Bronx only for a short time. We moved around an awful lot. We moved to Mount Vernon on MacQuestin Parkway near the Metro North train station where my uncle, Gene Denota, owned a taxi cab company. From there we moved to Bleeker Street when I was just a baby. Then in 1945, we moved to Locust Street, not far from MacQuestin Parkway.

Right across the street from us was a lot. That's where we used to play baseball. I remember my dad took several pictures of me. I was in a windup position as a pitcher with my leg way up in the air. I remember him telling me, "We'll send this to the Yankees." That was about 1948.

Bob Puccillo: "I remember wearing our '59 red and white championship WIAA jacket when I attended Arlington High School in my senior year and the kids didn't like that."

We lived on Locust Street until 1950 when we moved up to Carlyle, New York, near Cobleskill. My dad, Dan, wanted to open a restaurant there, so we moved with my mom, Susan, and my brother, Neil, who was seven years older than me.

We stayed there for a little over a year and then came back to Mount Vernon. My dad worked for Krug Baking Company on MacQuestin Parkway for a while. He also worked for Dugan's where he sold cakes and breads out of a truck. We moved to a house at 123 Beachwood Avenue, near Wilson Pool, off Lincoln Avenue and stayed there when I went to A.B. Davis High School.

As I mentioned, when I was about eight years old and living on Locust Street there was a lot right across the street from us. My dad took me there and taught me how to pitch. I remember him telling me that when the season was about to begin I should start off real slowly. Then, after a while, he had me bearing down. He showed me how to throw a curve, fastball, and a drop. So I had three pitches.

My dad wasn't really into sports except when he was a kid himself. He read a book about Bob Feller, the Hall of Fame Cleveland Indians pitcher. I remember the book vaguely which he eventually gave me. I wasn't much of a reader. But it had instructions about how to throw a fastball. My dad groomed me. He even took a peach basket and had me throw into it to improve my control. Baseball was my favorite sport back then. I tried basketball, but with baseball I could stand on the pitchers mound and just throw and then enjoy hitting.

Bob Puccillo

My mom, in the early 40s, loved baseball. The New York Giants were her favorite team. She told me a story about when I was in kindergarten at Mount Carmel School and she took me out of class once. It was Ladies Day at the Polo Grounds. We were going. When we got there, she said that I was dawdling while she was pulling me. She turned to look at me and said, "Come on. Come on."

She had bumped into a man. She turned, looked up at the man, and shrieked, "Bing Crosby." Crosby looked at her, and she said he was so mad because he was trying to be incognito. Once she mentioned his name she said people rushed over to see him. He gave my mom a dirty look. And she never forgot that.

She sure loved baseball. I don't know how many times she took me to Giants games on the trolley over by Mount Carmel. That was my introduction to baseball.

I never followed baseball much but loved playing it. I didn't know the stats of major league ballplayers. I've been like that all my life. I would rather be a player.

I don't know if you remember, but at Hutchinson Field there used to be woman who was in charge of baseball teams. I think this was the Pee Wee League. This was around 1948 when I was eight years old. I remember going down there. She had a book with the names of all the players. She was in charge of everything. I have memories of playing there at the time. That was even before I played in the Little League. I was a pretty good pitcher and hitter on The Pirates in Little League. I remember there was a school not far from Hutchison Field with two ball fields.

I remember playing a game, and my dad was in the stands directing me what pitch to throw. He would signal by holding down his fingers, one hand over the other hand like a catcher would do. "One" would be for a fast ball, "two" for a curve, and "three" for a drop. I'd sneak a look over at him to see what I should throw. My coach never knew what I was doing.

I recall in Little League hitting a ball right behind second base. There was a hole in the ground there. The ball went right into the hole and the fielders couldn't get it out. I ended up on second base with a double.

After Little League I played in the Mount Vernon Pony League where I always pitched. My dad always told me that my brother, Neil, had a good fastball. Mine wasn't as good as his, and I had to rely on my curve ball and drop. I remember a championship game at Hutchinson Field where they put together an all-star team of players. A fellow named Harry was pitching and not doing very well. My manager had me warming up on the side. Harry kept pitching. I found out later that because of that game he ruined his arm and never could pitch again. I never got in the game.

At A.B. Davis, I went out for the high school team only in my junior year. I never played JV ball. I remember a few things about that '59 team. I remember hitting the longest ball I had ever hit in my life. We were playing on the road and I was pitching. I smacked the ball over the centerfielder's head and started circling the bases. I was a slow runner, and the centerfielder finally got the ball and threw it in. I rounded third and came home where I was tagged out at the plate.

I understand no one on that '59 team hit a home run that season. I almost did. I remember Coach Sywetz was so mad at the third base coach. He chewed him out saying, "You see how slow he was running why you didn't stop him at third? The guy can't run."

That has stuck in my mind all these years. That was my moment of glory. The guys on the team were telling me that it was too bad that I didn't score. I didn't care. I was so thrilled that I hit a ball that far. We did win the game.

I had a pretty good season that year. I won two games. I remember pitching relief in the bottom of the third inning of our third game. I shut down Nyack the rest of the way and we won. I also remember playing centerfield during Eddie Martin's no-hitter. But probably the best game I had was against New Rochelle when I pitched and we won 8-1. I threw a complete game and gave up three hits, striking out five and walking five. I remember the control I had that season. I had junk on the ball. My fastball wasn't that fast, but my curve and drop were good.

During the season, my parents moved to Hyde Park, New York where my dad went into the cookie selling business. I had to live with my brother on Mount Vernon Avenue, so I could finish my junior year at Davis before moving. I probably was forgotten by my teammates right after that junior season. I moved away from Mount Vernon and spent my senior year at Arlington High School in Hyde Park.

Bob Puccillo: "We moved to Locust Street where my dad took pictures of me winding up. He said he was going to send them to the New York Yankees."

I remember wearing our '59 red and white championship WIAA jacket at Arlington High School. Some of the kids there didn't like the idea that I was wearing it in the hallways in my senior year. But I was proud of it.

When I tried out for the Arlington High School baseball team in my senior year, I was told I couldn't play because I was 19 years old. They said I was too old. That really throttled my enthusiasm for playing baseball. I never played ball again.

We moved a great deal when we lived in Mount Vernon. The one picture I have in my mind about the city was when we moved to Beachwood Avenue. It was winter time and for some reason I woke up in the middle of the night. We lived on the third floor of a house, and I looked out the window. It was snowing. There was a guy in a car pulling another fellow on skis. I thought it was so neat. I could hear them talking. It's something that has always been in my mind.

While we were living in Mount Vernon, one of my father's baked goods customers was a house painter who was part of trio of guitar players back in the '30s. He was pretty good. I picked up the guitar but wasn't practicing because I was playing baseball. I told my dad that I wanted to play baseball and didn't want to play the guitar. I was about ready to give up the guitar.

So my dad, he was smart. He got hold of this guy and invited him to our house. My dad wanted him to convince me to play. He came over and played a boogie-woogie on the guitar. I said, "Can you teach me that?" He replied, "Sure, note for note."

That's all it took. From that point on, no one had to tell me to practice. I remember there used to be a music store across the street from the Bee Hive Restaurant on Fourth Avenue in Mount Vernon. That was around '57 or '58. That's where I heard my first Chet Atkins record. I said, "This guy is great."

I bought several of his records but really didn't know how he played the music. He played a special way that interested me. So once my dad's customer showed me how to play that way, I took off. I started buying Chet Atkins records and began copying his playing style.

Bob Puccillo: "I went out for the high school team only in my junior year and never played JV ball."

My father bought me a tape recorder and I began taping Atkins on the guitar. I'd slow down the recording so I could learn to play like him. I remember two friends coming over to my house on Beachwood Avenue. We started playing in the backyard. We were using an amplifier. All of a sudden people from blocks around heard the music and came by. This kind of spurred me to play and really weaned me away from playing baseball.

I still play in my basement studio. Through the years I've been with a number of bands, such as Lenny Frank and The Rhythm Rockers. We played colleges and for about three years at a place across the Hudson River called The Hasbrook Room near New Paltz.

I wanted to hit the road and become a guitar player. I remember making a tape on January 1, 1966, when a couple of friends came over, and we recorded the music in our home on Lister Drive in Hyde Park.

At the time, I was working in Hyde Park in a machine factory. While there, a fellow named Jim Doyle started talking to me. I remember quite a few guys made fun of him. They used to call him reverend and monsignor.

I asked him, "Why do they call you that?" He said, "I am a Jehovah's Witnesses." "What's that? I've never heard of it," I replied.

He started explaining it to me. He said, "You think you know how to play that guitar. Wait until King David comes back in the resurrection because he was a master musician." I said, "What are you talking about?" You see, I was Catholic.

He brought a *Bible* to work, and everyday he explained it to me. I thought it sounded so logical and reasonable. At that time, I was engaged to my future wife, Susan, who told me to stay away from him. "He doesn't seem bad," I told her.

Susan and I were married on June 18th in 1966. Eventually I became a Jehovah's Witness and in 1967 my wife became one also. We've been married for 42 years and Witnesses for 41.

While living in Hyde Park, I wanted to learn about electronics because I liked the guitar. I went to Dutchess Community College for a while and eventually went into the full-time ministry. I would go out and talk to people about the *Bible*. I hurt my back badly and had to change professions. I worked in the Arlington School District for nearly 33 years before retiring.

12 *Frank Fiore*

I was an active child. I was even put on a 20-foot rope leash to stop me from taking off or running into the street. During World War II, my extended family, consisting of my father, mother, grandmother, and Aunt Mary rented a house in Mount Vernon.

In 1949, we moved to a first floor apartment in a five-story walk-up building at 21 West Sidney Avenue. Nearby was a corner store, opposite that a grocery, a candy store, and on the fourth corner, a church. Basically, it was a church and three bookie shops.

It was a working class neighborhood where people were postmen, clerks like my dad, Gaetano, who was a property records clerk for Con Edison, and dress operators like my mother, Grace. My mother was deaf in one ear, and I always had to face her when I spoke so she could read my lips.

I'll tell you, Mount Vernon was a great place to grow up in. I wouldn't give up that neighborhood for any other. Everybody was friendly from the first floor to the fifth. If you did something wrong, your family knew it before the day was out. Cops would pass by all the time. We were always sitting outside. Whenever somebody got into trouble, the cops would come by and say, "We're going to take your name, and if we see the name again we're going to take you in."

That's so different from today when cops say, "Ok, come to the precinct, I'm going to book you." Everything is black and white today. Back then there was more compassion for everybody. It was all about "give the kid a second chance." Nobody ever bothered you. As kids we walked everywhere.

Frank Fiore: "I don't think that championship team was as good as our sophomore junior varsity club."

I was seven-years-old when we moved to the apartment. That's where I came in contact with many other kids my age like my buddies, Ernie Cioffi, John Sullivan, and Bob Synnott. We were inseparable and would spend the next 11 years together. My father worked on Saturday's and John and Bob lost their fathers. Ernie's dad was sick most of the time, so we were all on our own.

Next to the apartment was a rock-and-glass strewn lot, maybe 50-feet by 100-feet. That's where we started to play baseball. I think Ernie must have had the idea. We'd go down the block to the shoemaker and buy tennis balls and start throwing. I think that's why my arm was never strong because of those light balls.

Since there were four of us, we played a game called automatics. Each team had a pitcher and a catcher. Ground balls were outs. If the ball reached the first sidewalk it was a single, the street a double, the far sidewalk a triple, and if you hit the house across the street it was a home run. If you broke a window you ran like hell.

My family's apartment was on the first floor, next to home plate. A window was broken at least five times a year. Once I thought I'd be smart and open the window so a ball could go through the open window and not break the window pane. That backfired because we broke the upper pane. That was two broken windows. My father never complained about fixing them.

At ten, we learned that the Little League was having tryouts. I never had a baseball glove. An older friend of the family gave me one of his for the tryouts. It was about twice the size of my hand and had five fingers. There wasn't webbing between the fingers, so I had to catch the ball in the palm of my hand or it would fall out.

I didn't make the Little League, so I was put on a minor league team where I played shortstop. I remember teammates like Phil and Frank Cenname, Jack Williams, and Joel Mazzerella, whose grandfather was the manager of the team. Frank was our pitcher, a left hander. That meant a lot of ground balls were hit up the middle. I could field them, step on second, and throw to first for a double play. The next year my dad got a call from a Little League manager who wanted me to join his team. However, I had a hernia and couldn't play any sports. That ended my organized baseball experience for a while.

Ernie, John, Bob, and I still kept on playing our automatic fast pitch baseball. At 12, we entered the Mount Vernon Recreation Baseball League. We were just a ragtag team without coaches. We'd walk to Hutchinson Field or Baker Field to play. Our last year we played for the championship. I got two hits that day and scored the tying run. The game was tied until the bottom of the seventh inning. A fly ball was hit to our left fielder who was smoking and not paying attention. The ball went by him for a home run and we lost.

Frank Fiore: "I'll tell you, Mount Vernon was a great place to grow up in."

The following year the four of us switched to slow pitch ball. We had outgrown our lot. We were kicked out of Hartley Park because the balls we hit over the fence were landing near young children on swings or on the merry-go-round. We moved our game up to the A.B. Davis High School football field.

In the tenth grade, Ernie and I tried out for the A.B. Davis baseball team. By this time playing slow pitch ball destroyed my timing and swing. I sat on the junior varsity bench for most of the season. I played occasionally at second or first base. That summer we entered a team in the Police Athletic League where I got a chance to play shortstop on a regular basis.

The year 1959 was a fun year for baseball. Actually we had two fun years, our sophomore year and then our second year when we won the championship. I don't think that championship team was as good as our sophomore junior varsity club. In tenth grade, I remember Ernie Motta pitching and having that big curve ball where batters would duck as the ball curved over the plate for a strike. Then there was Tony Cioppa hitting those tremendous drives. Ernie wasn't as good a pitcher when he was a junior in high school. But we had Eddie Martin who picked it up. And we had a few other players who came on. The morale on that championship team was great. We had fun together. I remember singing on the bus. It was a loose club.

I also remember keeping the scorebook most of the time during that championship season along with Billy Cioppa. I'd bring news about the game to the sports desk at the Mount Vernon Daily Argus right where we played. The paper was on First Street and Second Avenue. I never got paid for being the correspondent. I'd bring the scorebook to the paper and sit with the writer. He'd ask about game highlights and summarize our conversation. I worked with the same writer all the time and got quite friendly with him. Once I remember getting a hit, probably my only hit of the entire summer rec season. In the write-up about the game, the sportswriter made a big deal about my hit because he knew me.

We couldn't follow up that championship '59 season when most of us turned seniors. We lost some good players because they had to work. I remember Teddy Cardasis hurting his knee and still coming out to play ball. He batted lefty instead of hitting right-handed. He'd get a hit and limp around the bases. He still might have hit over .400 for the season. He was just amazing.

During the spring of my senior year, I remember playing both hardball and softball at the same time. I'd play for A.B. Davis, finish that game, and then go play a fast-pitch softball game for The Columbians. I think that's why I was a better hardball hitter in my senior year because of the speed of the softball pitches. As a senior, I got the chance to start at shortstop. I was hitting and fielding well until we scrimmaged Pelham High School and its two All County players, Ralph Lembo and Dom Cecere. I was covering second base and stepped toward the pitcher's mound to complete the double play. As I planted my left foot in the ground Lembo slid into me. I sprained my left ankle and missed most of the remaining games that season.

I think I'm the only player on our championship team who married a girl he went out with in high school. Maria DiVito and I were in Ms. Cleveland's same homeroom class. Maria was the teacher's pest whereas I was considered the teacher's pet. Ms. Cleveland would say to Maria, "Why can't you be more like Frank and bring in your note when you're absent?" I took her to the Varsity Dance in our senior year. That's how we started dating. We went out twice and stopped dating. In September I took her out again. We've been married 44 years and have three children, Stephanie, Chris, and Frankie. Stephanie lives in Hopewell Junction, Chris in Yorktown, and Frankie in Eastchester. Both Frankie and Chris are high school teachers in Eastchester.

Frank Fiore: "I'm probably the only player on our team who married a classmate he went out with in high school."

I've had a varied working career. I started out in construction working for Maria's father. I couldn't see myself working as a laborer for the rest of my life, so I bought an Arthur Treacher cleaning service franchise. I then went into the office cleaning business. I got rid of the Arthur Treacher franchise and kept the office cleaning part-time. For 20 years I worked two jobs, office cleaning and my day job as a welfare worker in New York City. That gave me a chance to play on some pretty good softball teams at fields like the park at 125th Street on the FDR Drive, 110th Street on the West Side, at Randall's Island, and in the Bronx at Lehman College. I eventually got into data processing and began working for MCI in 1993. I've been with them ever since. Today the company is Verizon.

I remember my kids coming to watch me play in those games. I also remember at 33 and the first signs of slowing down. A ball would be hit up the middle. I'd stretch and reach down to grab the ball, put my hand in the glove, and then throw to first. My glove would be empty.

13 *Steve Matthews*

Football was my best sport in high school. I was a left-handed center on offense and also a defensive end. We didn't have a very good record, but I enjoyed it.

Playing football was completely different than playing baseball because it was extremely rough in practice and much more competitive on game day. It was violent. There were plenty of times when guys were kicked off the team and didn't come back. There were fistfights in practice. It was the complete reversal of what it was like to play baseball at A.B. Davis.

I remember Bill Sywetz who was the line coach in football. He came up to most of us when we were sophomores and said, "If you want to play as a junior, you have to do something to stay in shape." It was either track and field or baseball in the spring.

I told him I would play baseball. So I went out for the baseball team and quickly saw that all the guys were far better ball players than I was. They played a lot more baseball growing up than I did.

But you know what; I immediately saw that it was a different type of team than our football team.

Football was a violent sport even then. There was more competition. There were a lot more skirmishes and fights on the field. Baseball was the cerebral game. You had a bunch of fellows who were really nice guys. So I got into the baseball thing and started playing first base.

Steve Matthews, left, and Ricky Libenson at Camp Ramaquois.

I think I played one or two games, it didn't matter. We had this team with Tony Cioppa, Teddy Cardasis, Tom Ambrosino, Lenny Henderson, Nicky Giordano, and Bruce Fabricant. They were all good ballplayers.

Every time Ernie Motta pitched, we seemed to win during our junior varsity season. Every time Gene Masucci or somebody else pitched, we either split or lost. So we had this team that really played well. I think our club ended up 7-2 or something like that.

Early that season, Sywetz, because he was new at coaching baseball, didn't quite understand who was good and who wasn't good. So he put me at first base. I played in a couple of pre-season JV games against Mount St. Michael. I even hit a double.

It wasn't until we played a few more games that Sywetz realized that there was a lot better talent out there than me.

So when I got on the team I said, "This isn't so bad; I'm not playing, but these are nice guys." I went out and shagged a few fly balls and got a little exercise. Being the screw-up that I was anyway, I didn't have to go home and study. This was really a nice place to be in nice weather.

So then we moved on to our junior year. We put this core of Cardasis, Ambrosino, Cioppa, Giordano, Motta, and Fabricant in with the seniors, Eddie Martin, Neil Arena, Mike Abrams, and John Fortier. It meshed into a pretty nice team. I looked at the team as an outsider while sitting on the bench and said, "This team has got some possibilities".

As the season moved along I realized that we were going to be tough to beat. Then I began watching something in athletics that kind of registered with me for the rest of my life. Guys in high school mature at different ages. I watched Ernie Motta, who was unbelievable as a sophomore but couldn't get anybody out in his junior year. He had come to the point where he had matured and everyone else caught up with him physically. I watched him split his six starts.

The star of the team was Eddie Martin. Not only could Eddie pitch, he also played shortstop and was a very solid singles and doubles hitter. He had this *herky-jerky* batting motion. Neil Arena, Jimmy Gross, and Bruce Fabricant shared second base when Eddie was at shortstop.

Tony Cioppa also was a good hitter. I can still see the home run he smacked as a sophomore into the creek deep at Hutchinson Field. The guy with the most talent was Teddy Cardasis.

Looking back, the one who impressed me the most was Tom Ambrosino. Tommy had real good hand-to-eye coordination and could hit the ball to all fields. I don't remember what he batted. It must have been well over .300. Tommy was one of those guys who came on and was better as a junior than he was as a sophomore. He was a good guy and played a fine first base. He even made honorable mention All-County.

In my opinion, Eddie had decent stuff, not great stuff a decent fastball, not a great fastball. But Eddie had something that has always been a key to pitching. He got the ball over the plate, and he always kept it low.

If you look at the scorecards when he pitched, there were a lot of ground balls. And if this team had one thing, it was defense. We turned double plays. There were a lot of force outs at second base. We made very few errors.

The team really won on Eddie's pitching, his ability to get the ball over the plate and not putting a lot of guys on base with walks. He made people beat the ball into the ground because, let me tell you, we had a bad hitting team.

I don't think we even came close to hitting .280 as a team. We had some timely hits. But after Ambrosino, Cardasis, Cioppa and Martin, it was kind of difficult. Occasionally, Mike Abrams and Nicky Giordano would come up with a key hit. But Arena and Fabricant were kind of pedestrian hitters.

So we really had a team based on about four players who could hit the ball. But we won that '59 championship with defense.

The blending of juniors and seniors was faultless. Everybody got along. We had a good time. It didn't matter who you were, what race you were, what religion you were. I never heard an argument.

Here's a postscript immediately after winning the championship. Martin, his friend Dennis O'Keefe, Mike Abrams, and I went to a little gin mill on the corner of Lincoln Avenue and Wolf's Lane in Pelham. I never drank before. They started drinking beers. I had to drink something that tasted decent, so I had a Vodka Collins. It was about 4:30 or 5:00 in the afternoon and we left at about 6:30. Abrams dropped me off at home where I went right upstairs. The room was spinning. That was the first time I ever was drunk.

I was born in Newark, New Jersey. My father, Nathan, was a veterinarian during World War II. He had a choice of either going into the military or becoming a meat inspector. He chose to become a veterinary meat inspector in Dubuque, Iowa, and later in the Chicago stockyards. After the war he came back east since he was born in Yonkers.

He bought an animal hospital and eventually bought another one, which he ran in Mount Vernon. It was right next to A.B. Davis High School on Gramatan Avenue. Our family including my dad, my mother, Sarah, and brother, Jeffrey, lived in a three-family house next door to the hospital.

Steve Matthews: "Steve and I played a lot of football together, which I know was his better sport."

I went to Lincoln Elementary School beginning in kindergarten and was there until the fifth grade when we moved to a single-family home at 25 Brookfield Road, a one minute walk to Baker Field where there used to be several ball fields. The fields and tennis courts are gone, and it's now the site of Mount Vernon High School.

I don't recall having many catches with my dad. But I remember Larry Briglia, Bruce Fabricant, and I playing in the Lincoln playground on a hard macadam surface. That was my earliest recollection of having a catch.

My memories of any kind of sport were based around the school yard, whether it was at Lincoln or Wilson Elementary School, later known as Traphagen. The school yards were where we learned to play ball.

It was basketball in the winter in Mount Vernon recreation leagues at Traphagen or at the Mount Vernon YMHA and softball and baseball in the spring. In the summer I went to Camp Ramaquois in Pomona, NY, where it was softball, basketball and soccer.

The big thing at school was playing softball at noon. I remember those games vividly, playing with Bob Weiner, Alan Brown, Richie Shapiro, and Bruce Fabricant. We would run home and grab a sandwich and get back to the playground in 15 to 20 minutes.

I remember playing softball games using only half the field. We played with Mike Abrams and Jimmy Gross, who were a grade ahead of us, and with Jimmy Anchin and Bob Trupin, who were a class behind. The age differences didn't matter. We played ball together almost every day.

I did try out for the Little League when I was 12 but didn't make it. Actually, my favorite sport was really basketball, but I was best at football. I liked to hit people. My weakest sport was baseball. Although I was a pretty decent softball player, I never really could hit a baseball. Maybe it was the hitch in my swing.

I remember we used to play for the Dukes in the Mount Vernon recreation league. I was a left-handed catcher. I had a right-handed mitt and switched it around to my non-throwing hand.

I recall getting up at 6:30 in the morning for a 9:30 game. We had an umpire, Jake, who was an old man. We would scream at Jake saying, "What a terrible call!" Of course, there was only one umpire. He stood behind the pitcher and would have to umpire all the bases, the outfield, and call balls and strikes.

Looking back, I think it was a little unfair ripping into him. But those were fun times. Those were the years in junior high school when on a Saturday you left the house at 8:00 in the morning and didn't come back until 5:00 at night. You managed to grab a sandwich somewhere at a luncheonette. Whatever the season was, you played ball all day.

I remember meeting many kids who later would become my friends in high school. You see, Little League games were played at Baker Field, which was near my house. I used to watch guys like Cardasis, Martin, Giordano, and Ambrosino play. Most of them lived in the Nichols area and came across town to play ball. I didn't know many of them until I started playing basketball against them in junior high school.

Most of them, like Ernie Motta, were Little League players of some note. I didn't see them play in the Pony League. But I watched them when they played for the Paramounts, the team Dorothy Bourne sponsored. They played doubleheaders down at Memorial Field where I would go on a warm spring or summer day.

It was fabulous growing up in Mount Vernon. It was the sweetest of times. I tell my kids that all the time. The '50s was a great era to grow up in the New York area. It was the best, the finest, the most peaceful of times.

Where I lived, we went basically from being in an all-white, largely Jewish elementary and junior high school to a completely integrated high school. People got along with each other. People mixed in high school. I didn't think there was much in the way of racism. They were just good times.

Growing up, I had two idols in my life, my father and Jackie Robinson. The Dodgers were my team. I was old enough to understand exactly what was happening. Before Martin Luther King, there was Jackie Robinson. He probably did more than anyone else to focus attention on the unfairness of American society. He had the ethics, the morals, and guts that all Americans should have. He was a tremendous American. I loved the way he played. I loved his moxie. He had a lot of talent. That led me to a lifelong love affair with the Dodgers.

Steve Matthews

I am still a huge Dodgers fan today. I remember the arguments we had growing up. We would argue at the playground or in later years at Albanese's Restaurant in Tuckahoe. I would ask, "Who is the better centerfielder Snider, Mays or Mantle?" Then the arguments began.

I still reflect on those moments in 1955 when the Dodgers finally won their first World Series after losing in 1952 and 1953. In 1955 they came back when Johnny Podres led them to a seventh game victory. That was a tremendous moment in my life.

I'll never forget where I was. I was out on the playground at Traphagen. We had a late gym class. Our gym teacher, Anthony Soldano, allowed us to bring radios to class. We were standing outside in the afternoon listening as Brooklyn won the game on the pitching of Podres and the great catch by Sandy Amoros off Yogi Berra.

I used to go to Ebbets Field in Brooklyn with two friends, Alan Brown and Mike Rubin. We took the F bus or got a ride to 241st Street in the Bronx, the end of Mount Vernon. We walked across the street. That was the last stop on the subway line. I remember taking five or six bologna sandwiches on the subway and sitting on those hard straw seats.

It was about a 2¼ hour ride to that little dingy bandbox of a place. We would sit in upper box seats in the first row that would cost maybe three dollars. It was a great place to watch a game. I recall going to an opening day game to see a 17- or 18-year-old Don Drysdale pitch for the Dodgers.

Those were fun times in Mount Vernon. That junior varsity and the championship team in '59 were just special. I wore that red and white WIAA championship jacket probably until my junior year in college at Kansas State University.

After college I married my wife, Judy, who died October 28, 2000. She was my partner in life, my partner in business. I have been in the fastener business for 42 years now, and I'm pretty much committed for another couple of years. We have two children, a daughter who works for Morgan Stanley and a son who is an art historian and professor at John Jay College in Manhattan.

I recall going out for the baseball team again as a senior in 1960. I remember putting on my uniform. It was a nice warm early April day. I went down the ball field to shag fly balls and said, "You know what, I think I've had it with organized ball."

I went up to Coach Sywetz at the end of the practice and handed in my uniform and told him I was going to do other things. One of the most enjoyable things was going down to Traphagen every evening, right after we finished eating, to play softball.

We played from 6 o'clock until it was too dark to see the ball. We usually played two 7-inning games. That was just pure fun. The field was all dirt with some gravel in the outfield. There were no barriers so if the ball got by you, you could run forever to catch up with it.

There were trees overhanging third base. So if you were a pull hitter, you just kept banging the ball into the trees forever. If you hit the ball to right field, and I was a lefty, the roll would roll all the way to the school which was about 600 feet away.

We had fun times. And do you know something; I didn't even know what my high school team did in that senior year. When I took off my uniform that spring, it was the last time I ever put a uniform on in an organized sport.

14 *Jimmy Gross*

When I was seven or eight, I was playing softball with guys who were fifteen years old. I was there because they were friends with my brother, Eddie, who was six years older than me. But I could play with them at that age. Starting off I played right field.

The Traphagen schoolyard, where everybody went, was right down the block from my house at 15 Lexington Avenue. Actually, it was called Wilson School then. We moved to Mount Vernon from the Bronx when I was one.

I remember there was a famous green box there where they kept all the bats and balls for our Sunday morning game. Those were pretty good days. If you hit a long fly ball and made the basketball court blacktop, which was probably about 200 feet away, that was some shot. We had a reunion about 20 years ago with a lot of the old guys from Mount Vernon who played three-on-three or four-on-four basketball and softball there.

My first hardball team was the Mighty Midgets. We played at Baker Field. Guys on the team like Jeff Bluestein, Ira Deutsch, and Jack Rothenberg were two and three years older than me. Then a few years later I organized and named a team called the Scorpions. We even had jackets. Mike Abrams and I pitched. Also on the team were fellows like Mike Richman, Steve Danetz, Skippy Baum, and Donnie Robinson. There were about nine or ten of us. We had been together since kindergarten.

Jimmy Gross

We were good. We were part of the Mount Vernon recreation league. I remember going to City Hall to get field permits. It was terrific. Parents never got involved, which probably was the best thing that happened looking back on things. It's not like that today.

I never played in the Little League since all the kids in our area went to camp in the summer. I didn't know a soul who played Little League ball.

When I got to A.B. Davis, I went right to the varsity as a sophomore. Mr. Halstead, the coach, heard about me because he coached Bob DeLemos, who graduated four years ahead of me. Bob's father owned a summer camp where I went. So Mr. Halstead knew me as soon as I got to high school. I started in right field and then played second base. We had a good team with John VonBargen and Stan Cherson pitching. So I played as a sophomore on the varsity. That's where I think I peaked.

In the beginning of my junior year I broke my ankle playing basketball. That kept me out of spring baseball. Then senior year came along and something happened that is almost embarrassing. I went to Florida with my parents during Easter vacation. I never thought about staying home. In those days, you didn't tell your parents you were going to stay home. I didn't think pre-season baseball was that important. Today, if I had a choice again, I wouldn't have gone to Florida.

There was a new varsity coach in my senior year. I played in only three games during that championship season. I started the first game at third base when we lost to Nyack 5-4. I walked and scored a run. The next game against Clarkstown we tied 3-3 and I was at third again. I remember Eddie Martin's no-hitter against New Rochelle. In the fifth inning, I caught a line drive and fired home to nab the runner at the plate to help save Eddie's no-hitter.

Like an idiot, I quit the team right after that. It was a childish thing I did and I regret it. That's the way it was. It wasn't like today. It wasn't a big deal.

I actually enjoyed playing basketball as much as baseball. In fact, I had a better time playing basketball. Neil Arena and I had some great times playing basketball in high school. That was really fun. On the team we had Jordan Hollingsworth, Chico Coleman, Jimmy Schneider, and Richie Shapiro. If we lost and I didn't do well, I wouldn't talk to anybody. Those games were tremendous.

Earlier, we were the only team that ever beat Washington Junior High School when we played basketball for Traphagen. I never lost to them in two years. That was in seventh and eighth grade. They hated us. I remember Mark Klein who played for us. He wasn't very good, but he was 6-feet 2-inches tall when he was 12 years old. I still have a picture that Mike Abrams gave me of us winning the Mount Vernon Midget League championship when we were 13 years old.

Growing up in Mount Vernon was the best. Life was simpler. Mount Vernon was a pretty special place. Then you didn't see the arrogance and entitlement you see in today's kids.

After high school I graduated from Union College and went to graduate school for a year at the American Institute of Foreign Trade, now called The Thunderbird School. Viet Nam was heating up when I got out in July, 1964. I was lucky enough to get in the Coast Guard. About a week after I started basic training, the football coach came around and asked who of us played football in college.

I raised my hand. I then called my father and said, "Pop, I have a chance to get out of everything if I can make this team."

"Go ahead," he said. He really didn't want me to play football. My dad, Saul, was an accountant and earlier was a catcher for Commerce High School in New York City.

So I tried out for the team and made it. My life was at stake. As soon as I made it, I'm out of the barracks and into new barracks with the drill team band and the football team. At the end of the season I became a gym instructor for three months. That was my six months in the service. It was a good experience, a lot of fun.

My wife, Marsha, gave me a present for my 45th birthday, a trip to the Dodgers fantasy camp in Vero Beach, Florida. My brother lives in Vero and I was a big Giants fan growing up. So to put on a Dodgers uniform was something else. It was fantastic. I learned more there in a week than I did in 15 years. We played with Carl Erskine, Clem Labine, and Ralph Branca. Branca and I hit it off because we were both from Mount Vernon and went to Davis High School. I did that for four years in a row.

Then I saw an ad in the local paper about a hockey league. That was in 1986. I always wanted to do play hockey, but I didn't even know how to skate. So I went to hockey camp up in Canada for 12 years starting in 1989. I organized the youth hockey group in Larchmont and we would take about 30 kids every summer to Canada.

I still play Monday nights for nearly two hours at the

Hommacks Park Ice Rink, which is five minutes from my house in Larchmont. Then we have beer afterwards. I used to play two nights a week. Then I had my hips replaced. I'm not very good anymore. I'm a goalie. We have a nice bunch of guys. There isn't any checking. I talk to some of the guys like we're in kindergarten.

I say, "We all have to work the next day, so no head cases out there." My career has been in the commercial real estate industry.

Marsha and I have two boys, Tim and Pete. Both went to Salisbury Prep School where Pete played football, hockey and lacrosse. He later became captain of Union's lacrosse team in his junior and senior year. What's great is that Pete plays a lot of hockey now. He plays with the Union guys in Stamford and with my team on Monday night. The best part is that he carries my hockey bag.

15 *Charlie Siegel*

Basically, I was A.B. Davis's Pelham pitcher. I was on the mound in several pre-season games against Pelham Memorial High School in our championship season.

That was the extent of my high school varsity baseball career. But it wasn't the end of my pitching career by a long shot.

How about throwing a no-hitter at the age of 30? That's what I did for the barnstorming Mount Vernon Paramounts against a White Plains team. I don't think any of my high school teammates played organized baseball for that long, let alone pitch a no-hitter.

As you can imagine, I loved the game.

It bothered me not playing on that '59 high school team. No one likes sitting on the bench. You think you can do what the guy out there is doing. It was annoying to sit. But that was the way it was.

I played junior varsity baseball for Coach Cliff Tetro at Davis. I remember in my senior year, Coach Sywetz really liked Eddie Martin, who was a control pitcher. I wasn't. As a youngster, I threw a fastball and, believe it or not, a change up, like a slip pitch. That was actually my out pitch. My fast ball wasn't fast enough even in high school.

I'm not sure if I stayed on the squad for the entire season. I may have gone over to run track that senior year. I ran the half-mile during the spring and cross country in the fall. I recall that in my sophomore year I was 13th or 14th in the Westchester sectionals. I was a pretty good runner until I started smoking and driving.

Charlie Siegel: "Basically I was A.B. Davis' Pelham Memorial High School pitcher in several pre-season games."

I never gave up on baseball and played a lot of it after graduating high school all the way into my thirties. You see, after high school I finally found control of my pitches. I was able to get people out, so I continued to play either as a pitcher or first baseman.

After high school, I played for the Sluggers, a Mount Vernon team run by a man named Pappy Brooker. I shared the pitching with his son, Ron Brooker. Years earlier, my brother, Steve, played for Pappy. I remember playing in the city intermediate league championship game.

The Paramounts was another team I pitched for. I remember being on the mound in a game in Byrum, Connecticut. A Cleveland Indians scout was there. After the game he came up to me and said, "Keep up the good hitting." You see, during the game, I hit a 350-foot shot to the opposite field. He didn't like my pitching at all. I knew then that it was all over.

Neither the Sluggers nor Paramounts had an A.B. Davis high

school player on the squad. There were some fellows from the other Mount Vernon High School, Edison Tech, on the both clubs. Bobby Devanzo, who used to play professional football for the Mount Vernon Eagles football team, was one. There was also Louie Oria and Andy Montague. We had a great shortstop, Phil DeFillippo, who hurt his hand at work, which kept him from signing a professional contract.

In later years I played for the Yonkers' Mets and for Regan's of Westchester, an office furniture company that sponsored the team and provided uniforms.

In 1971 when I was 30 years old, I pitched a no-hitter for Regan's against the Nepperhan Bucks in a White Plains twilight baseball game at Rec Park. We won 16-0. I was in control that night, striking out 10 and walking only three batters.

That was quite a few years after I first began playing baseball. I was born in Mount Vernon and lived on 8 Hartley Avenue near the circle on Gramatan Avenue. There was a row of houses behind Gramatan Avenue right in front of the high school. That's where I lived.

My dad, Irving, was an accountant and wasn't interested in sports. His real name was Isadore. Would you believe he changed it from Isadore to Irving?

For 35 years, he was an accountant for the unemployment insurance division of New York State. My mother, Henrietta, worked for Scharco, a baby carriage manufacturing company in Mount Vernon. It was owned by my friend Ira Scharaga's father. Later, she took a test and went to work for the Mount Vernon public library. My brother, Steve, who graduated from A.B. Davis in 1954, retired from IBM and is working on keeping the library alive.

When I was six and seven years old, Tommy Smith, Freddie Diringer, and I started playing ball in a parking lot in the back of the house. That's where my baseball career began. A little later, we started going up to the high school to play since we lived so close to it. It was just a matter of climbing all those steps on Gramatan Avenue. The best I can say is that we played a disorganized brand of baseball until I was older and joined organized leagues.

Siegel threw a no-hitter at the age of 30 for the Mount Vernon Paramounts.

During the summers my family went to vacation in the country in Columbia County, New York. That's when I got my first baseball glove.

Do you remember S&H Green Stamps? They were trading stamps popular in the United States between the 1930s and late 1980s. Customers would receive stamps at the checkout counter of supermarkets, department stores, and gas stations. We could redeem the stamps for products in a catalog.

That's what my father did for me. He got me my first glove, a black first baseman's mitt, with Green Stamps. The glove came right out of the Green Stamps catalog. There was a problem though. The glove was for a right hander. I was a left hander. As you can tell, my dad wasn't a big sports fan. Nevertheless, I used that mitt for a while.

By the time I was in the sixth and seventh grade, we were

playing a more serious brand of baseball. Our games were at Baker Field in the Mount Vernon recreation league, and I remember that John Fortier, our high school teammate, was my centerfielder.

Baseball wasn't my only sport. I was big as a youngster. By the time I was 13 years old I was six-feet tall, so I was a center on all the basketball teams. I wasn't a very good one. But big is better at whatever level of basketball. Back then I would play quite a bit at the YMHA on Oakley Avenue, which was close by our house.

We also had a team called the Renegades in the Mount Vernon recreation midget league. Junior high basketball also was very popular. We had a pretty good team at Nichols. Playing along side me was Scharaga, Ira Zilin, and Carl Viggiano. Another team that comes to mind was the Scorpions. I remember playing with Ronnie Corwin, Bob Dobrish, Mike Abrams, Steve Danetz, Mike Richman, Bob Levine, and Alan Cooper. We had some pretty tough games against fellows I went to junior high school with like Gene Masucci, Viggiano, and Shaun Friary.

Mount Vernon was a friendly town with friendly people. I was on the committee that planned the 50th anniversary of our 1959 high school graduating class. So, even to this day, there are hundreds of people who I can reminisce with about that era.

After graduating from Davis, I went to Clark University for a short time. I quickly decided to go to work because I wasn't a great studier. By 21, I was in the office equipment business with an older partner and a high school classmate, Bob Burack. Bob eventually had enough with the business, while I stuck with it for 20 years in White Plains. I eventually sold it when electronics were first introduced.

For the last 25 years I have been working for a high school classmate, Ken Lazar, who operates Lazar Consulting Associates in White Plains. The commute to work from Rockland County is rough. I've lived across the Tappan Zee Bridge with my wife for the past 23 years.

16 *The 1959 Season at a Glance*

Nyack Beats Davis 5-4 in Season Opener

An opening day 5-4 loss to Nyack offers little indication about A.B. Davis High School's '59 season. Despite outhitting Nyack, the Hilltoppers fell one run short. Junior Ernie Motta gave up four hits and picked up the loss. Tony Cioppa, Nick Giordano and Eddie Martin each banged out two hits. Giordano and Martin were the only Hilltoppers to appear in all 16 games.

Clarkstown and Davis Tie 3-3

A single and a double-steal netted Davis two runs in the top of the seventh inning against Clarkstown, enough to tie the game 3-3 which was called because of darkness. Martin started and went six innings, giving up 3 runs, the only time he didn't complete a game all season. Over his next 18 innings, Martin would give up only one run.

Davis Edges Nyack 7-6

Davis avenged its opening game loss by beating Nyack 7-6 on the road. Richie Shapiro started and lasted two innings. Bob Puccillo relieved and picked up the win. Giordano drove in the first two runs. Martin tripled; the club's only triple all season.

First baseman Tom Ambrosino began his season-long hot hitting, going 3-3. Ambrosino captured honorable mention All-County honors. His .379 batting average led the club.

Davis Tops Commerce 1-0

A double by Lenny Henderson gave Davis its second win, a 1-0 shutout over Commerce High School of Yonkers. Martin tossed a four-hit shutout for his first win. He would go on to become the top right handed pitcher in Westchester County in compiling a 7-0 record. He was selected to the 1959 All-Westchester first team. Besides tying for the team lead in games played, he led the club in scoring nine runs and at bats with 50.

Rye Garnets Belt Davis 9-3

Davis saw its three game winning streak snapped by Rye High School, losing 9-3 on the road. The middle of the batting order, Martin, Cioppa, Giordano and Teddy Cardasis combined for 5 hits. Cardasis went on to bat .350 for the season while picking up All-County honorable mention honors. He led the club with 14 hits.

Martin No-Hits New Rochelle 1-0

Martin tossed a 1-0 no-hitter against New Rochelle. In the third inning, Cioppa doubled to drive in Henderson with the game's only run. Jimmy Gross snared a line drive and doubled up a running to keep Martin's no-hitter alive in the fifth inning. An inning earlier, Giordano scrambled over the left field boundary logs at Hutchinson Field to make a spectacular catch.

Davis Beats White Plains 5-2

Davis picked up its second Westchester Interscholastic Athletic Association win in beating White Plains 5-2 at home. Motta went all the way to pick up his first win. Davis clinched the game in the fifth inning on Giordano's double that drove in two runs.

Davis Edges Yonkers 2-1

Martin's four-hitter kept Davis undefeated in WIAA league play. The Hilltoppers stopped Yonkers 2-1. In the fifth inning, second baseman Bruce Fabricant walked. Henderson hit sharply to the Yonkers first baseman who failed to come up with the ball. Fabricant, running on the pitch, came in to score the winning run.

Davis Tops White Plains 4-3

Davis remained unbeaten in WIAA play, beating White Plains 4-3, with four runs in the top of the sixth inning as Martin stretched his record to 4-0.

Roosevelt Hands Davis First WIAA Loss 5-1

Davis suffered its first and only WIAA loss of the season, losing at home to Roosevelt High School of Yonkers 5-1. Cardasis singled in the bottom of the seventh inning, his second hit of the game, and drove in John Fortier for Davis' only run. Davis wouldn't lose another game, putting together a season-ending six game winning streak.

Davis Shuts Out Saunders 3-0

The race for the lead in the WIAA got caught up in a tie between Davis and Saunders High School of Yonkers after the Hilltoppers shut out Saunders 3-0 on Martin's four hitter, his fifth win in a row.

Davis Routs New Rochelle 8-1

Davis took over first place in the WIAA race with an 8-1 win over New Rochelle High School, behind the three-hit pitching of Puccillo. Singles by Martin, Cioppa, Ambrosino, and walks to Puccillo, Cardasis, plus a double by Neil Arena gave Davis six runs in the third inning. Davis ended league play 6-1. The Hilltoppers had to wait for Saunders to play Roosevelt. Saunders knocked off its Yonkers rival in the last game of the season to give Davis the league championship.

Davis Tops Lincoln 7-5

The Hilltoppers beat Lincoln High School of Yonkers 7-5 on 10 hits, the most the club registered all season. Davis would duplicate that with 10 hits against Edison Tech. Motta went the first five innings to pick up the win. Davis tied the game in the second inning on a squeeze bunt by Mike Abrams that scored Giordano. Davis took the lead in the third with five runs on singles by Martin, Cioppa, Cardasis, and Ambrosino, and a double by Abrams.

Davis Edges Suffern 3-2

Heads-up base running by outfielder Fortier led Davis to a 3-2 victory. Fortier stole two bases and reaching first on a walk. He slid home on a passed ball with the tie-breaking run. Martin went the distance to pick up his sixth win of the season.

Davis Routs Concordia 10-4

Third baseman Abrams blasted two doubles to drive in three runs as Davis beat Concordia 10-4. His three doubles would lead the club in '59. This was the only game Davis scored 10 runs. Davis however did not hit a home run all season. Motta picked up the victory, his third.

Davis Ends Season with 6-0 Victory over Edison Tech

Martin shut out cross-town Mount Vernon rival Edison Tech 6-0 to end the 1959 season. He finished the season with a 7-0 record including three shutouts and a no-hitter. Davis had eight hits, with Abrams and Cardasis getting two apiece.

A.B. Davis High School, Gramatan Avenue, Mount Vernon, NY

17 *Remembering Mount Vernon*

Here's to long forgotten times and places and things of yesterday. Here's to spring that ushered in the school band parade down Fourth Avenue. With trumpets blaring and Davis and Edison twirlers strutting, the parade was a rite of passage. Motorcycle cops kept spectators back who were lined five and six deep on the sidewalk.

How about taking a trolley at the intersection of Fifth Avenue and First Street to attend the football game of the year at Memorial Field? It was Mount Vernon's equivalent to the Army-Navy battle, only it was Davis vs. Edison Tech on Thanksgiving morning.

Here's to Saturday afternoons at the Biltmore Theater with its three feature length movies, most of them westerns and horror films, ten cartoons, a super hero serial, and at least one short subject. Thursday nights were special because it was Dish Night at the Biltmore. If you weren't at the Biltmore, then there's a good chance you went to RKO Proctors, Loews, the Embassy or the Parkway Theater. And here's to holding hands and stealing a kiss in the darkened balcony of RKO Proctors and rubbing your eyes when leaving the movies on a sunny Saturday afternoon. And here's to the old Wartburg Lover's Lane, now the site of Mount Vernon High School's athletic field.

Here's to Treasure Isle where many a young woman received

at least one engagement, shower, or wedding gift, and to two more landmarks on Fourth Avenue Genungs and The Fair. Where else but at The Fair could you find almost any household item or Santa Claus sitting near the second floor window waving to shoppers below.

Here's to the bargains galore at the three five and dime stores on Fourth Avenue, Green's, Woolworth's, and Kresge's. And if you couldn't find it there, Duff's on Gramatan Avenue was the place to go.

Here's to your first baseball glove bought at Tom Godfrey's, first located in the Proctor Building and later on Fourth Avenue. Barish's on Gramatan Avenue was the place for any stationary needs or school supplies. And for the music lovers there was always Norman's or Brodbeck's.

The only important second floor on all of Gramatan Avenue was Joe Mari's pool hall. Down the street there was Harry's at the circle where you bought ice cream packed in cardboard containers. For those from the south side there was the famous Sugar Bowl soda fountain at the corner of Sanford Boulevard and South Fifth Avenue. And who didn't love those egg creams made by Ruby at his luncheonette on East Lincoln Avenue.

Ferrara's Bakery on the Sidney Avenue hill made the best Italian bread this side of Italy. Would Chinese take out come from any other restaurant than Poppa Wong's on Gramatan Avenue? The Bon Ton dairy on South Fourth Avenue sold fresh butter from large wooden tubs while fruits and vegetables were purchased at Sepe's Market on Third Street, Daniello's on South Fourth Avenue, or Ben Nat's on Grand Street in Fleetwood. And here's to the best pastrami and corned beef sandwiches in the city at Gelb's Deli, of course.

For the sweet tooth's there was Fanny Farmer's Candy Store on Fourth Avenue. Turning to times gone by, the ladies bought their dresses at Bromley's on Fourth Avenue. You couldn't miss Bromley's with its huge street clock right outside the door. If you were looking for shoes, you went to Fleetwood and Alfonso's, and if was flowers there was the Cardasis Flower Shop on Gramatan Avenue.

Here's to your mother who took you to the Federal Bake Shop on Fourth Avenue where a portion of the back wall was glass and you could watch the bakers ice their freshly baked cakes. On Third Street there was the Francis Edwards Ice Cream Parlor with its peanut roasting machine in the front window. Right next door was Johnny's Pizzeria where Johnny held court.

The choice is yours. Where was the best pizza? Was it Johnny's or Decca on First Street or Vera's Pizzeria on Gramatan Avenue? Delicious buns and cakes came from the Daylight Bakery on First Street or from the Chester Heights Bakery. Great coffee rings could be found at the Coronet on Gramatan Avenue and crumb buns and crullers at Schwerger's Bakery near Scott's Bridge.

Here's to the many breakfast choices you had. Remember Stanley's on First Street, Bickford's and the Waldorf on Fourth Avenue, Ruby's Luncheonette on Lincoln Avenue near Pelham, the luncheonette on the corner of Gramatan Avenue and Grand Street, and the Cozy Corner in Chester Heights where you could order a nickel coke and nurse it all day long.

And where else but at the storefront window of Crystals on South Fourth Avenue could you find the best frozen custard ever made. The Broken Drum on Gramatan was a favorite for A.B. Davis kids. But for the quintessential ice cream sundae there was no place like the Bee Hive on Fourth Avenue. Here's to the huge chocolate eggs and bunnies displayed on the soda fountain there for Easter Sunday.

If you wanted delicious sandwiches, wedges, and potato salads there was no equal to Knopp's Deli at the circle. A lunch-time ritual at A.B. Davis was a roast beef wedge and Orange Crush soda. Here's a time to raise a cup of cheer to Mrs. Knopp and her salads and to her husband, Mr. Knopp, a true gentleman.

And here's to spring and summers spent at Brush Park, Baker Field, and baseball diamonds at schools all across the city, and also at Hartley Park. And for real nostalgia there were winter Saturday afternoons at the Mount Vernon Roller Skating Rink on Lincoln Avenue and coffee across the street at the Vee Diner.

Here's to the barber, Mr. D'Ambrosio, who got off of the D bus everyday in Chester Heights walked in to the barbershop and turned on his radio to listen to opera while giving you a haircut.

Here's to the wheels from discarded carriages that helped you make wagons out of old fish boxes from Oscar Abel & Sons Fish Market. And what about making scooters with the wheels from old roller skates and the fruit and vegetable boxes from Sepe's Market?

Here's to your youthful years spent at the Boy's Club on North Tenth Avenue. Depending on your age there were the Peewees, Juniors, Intermediates and Seniors. The director Mr. Kullen and his assistant Sal Celestina kept everyone on the straight and narrow. For special summers, there was Camp Rainbow, the Boy's Club camp in Hopewell Junction.

And who can ever forget the YMHA on Oakley Avenue and its dances and basketball, especially on Sunday afternoons. Here's to the clubs there that we left behind, The Cheyennes, The Dukes, OD and OBP, and Sub Debs. That's where many boys shot hoops for the first time under the watchful eye of Uncle Dave and Uncle Moe. The Y's Camp Willoway was the place to spend eight weeks of summer.

Are we hopelessly old fashioned remembering how we learned to dance at Teen Town on First Avenue and at the CYO at our Lady of Victory Church? On Thursday nights we met friends on Fourth Avenue where the stores stayed open until 9 pm.

Here's to the stoop of Katz's Grocery Store on North Sixth Avenue and North Street where we listened to weddings across the way at the National Guard Armory. Another favorite place for weddings was Turn Hall on Stevens Avenue. And three cheers for Mount Vernon's most recognizable landmark, the traffic circle at Gramatan and Lincoln Avenues.

Here's to the peddlers coming through our neighborhoods selling fruits and vegetables and even sharpening knives and to the bells each summer that would chime from the Bungalow Bar and Good Humor trucks. That's when we dove into the cool water at the Wilson Woods Pool and waited each June for the Saint Anthony Feast which originated on South Seventh Avenue and Third Street and was later held on South Tenth Avenue.

Ah yes, we remember it all so well.

www.ingramcontent.com/pod-product-compliance
Lightning Source LLC
La Vergne TN
LVHW011235080426
835509LV00005B/516